剑桥国际英语口语速成（修订版）

主编：[美] 汤姆·肯尼（Tom Kenny）

[美] 琳达·吴（Linda Woo）

北京语言大学出版社
BEIJING LANGUAGE AND CULTURE
UNIVERSITY PRESS

CAMBRIDGE
UNIVERSITY PRESS

社图号 22074

北京市版权局著作权合同登记图字：01-2021-5786 号

图书在版编目 (CIP) 数据

剑桥国际英语口语速成．1：修订版 ／（美）汤姆·肯尼 (Tom Kenny),（美）琳达·吴 (Linda Woo) 主编．-- 2 版．-- 北京：北京语言大学出版社，2022.9
ISBN 978-7-5619-6134-6

Ⅰ．①剑… Ⅱ．①汤… ②琳… Ⅲ．①英语－口语－自学参考资料 Ⅳ．① H319.9

中国版本图书馆 CIP 数据核字 (2022) 第 147476 号

剑桥国际英语口语速成1（修订版）
JIANQIAO GUOJI YINGYU KOUYU SUCHENG 1 (XIUDING BAN)

项目策划：李 亮	责任编辑：王春雨	封面设计：张 娜	责任印制：周 燚

出版发行：北京语言大学出版社
社　　址：北京市海淀区学院路 15 号，100083
网　　址：www.blcup.com
电子信箱：service@blcup.com
电　　话：编 辑 部　8610-82300178
　　　　　发 行 部　8610-82303650/3591/3648
　　　　　北语书店　8610-82303653
　　　　　网购咨询　8610-82303908
印　　刷：天津嘉恒印务有限公司
版　　次：2013 年 12 月第 1 版　　2022 年 9 月第 2 版
印　　次：2022 年 9 月第 1 次印刷　　　　开　本：880 毫米 × 1230 毫米　1/16
印　　张：7.75　　　　　　　　　　　　字　数：202 千字
定　　价：49.00 元

PRINTED IN CHINA
凡有印装质量问题，本社负责调换。售后 QQ 号 1367565611，电话 010–82303590

出 版 说 明

《剑桥国际英语口语速成》（*Nice Talking with You*）是剑桥大学出版社出版的一套初级英语口语学习用书，由北京语言大学出版社原版引进。本套口语学习用书分为两个级别，每个级别由 12 个主题单元和 2 个复习单元组成，每个单元围绕一个日常生活、学习或工作中常见的话题，教给学习者不同的对话策略。本书为其中的级别 1。

本书的作者是谁？

本书是由来自日本名古屋外国语大学的汤姆 · 肯尼（Tom Kenny）教授及其同人基于大量的英语口语教学实践、对东亚国家英语学习者的深入了解和对他们英语口语学习规律的不断总结编著而成。鉴于亚洲英语学习者在英语口语学习中有很多共同的规律，因此本书也特别适合中国英语学习者使用。

本书有什么与众不同的地方？

本书不同于其他口语学习用书，不需要你记忆不同篇幅的对话内容，而是帮助你运用不同的对话策略进行真实的对话，谈论你自己或者你身边的亲朋好友。这些真实的对话策略在每种语言中都很常见，它们帮助你与他人之间建立起良好的关系，这也是这些对话策略最重要的功能。

本书如何帮助你学好英语口语？

- 你会用到一些以前可能学过但是在对话中从未使用过的词汇。
- 你会围绕一个容易讨论的话题，以限时对话的形式进行口语练习。
- 你会学会如何准备对话，并且练习注意倾听你和你的语伴所说的英语。
- 你会听到来自世界各地的人（英语母语者和非英语母语者）带有不同口音的真实的英语口语。
- 最重要的一点，你会掌握一些重要的短语或表达，让你的对话更流利、更自然，我们称之为"对话策略"。

本书学习的目标是什么？

当你学完本书时，你会自然、熟练地使用所有学会的对话策略，达到用英语与他人自然交流的目的。

每个单元的学习目标是什么？

通过每个单元的学习，你会学会使用一些新的对话策略，开口说英语。

每个单元都包含哪些部分？

本书分为 12 个主题单元，每个单元都有一系列精心设计、紧密联系的口语练习和活动。每个单元的模块和功能如下所示：

🔲 Likes and dislikes（喜欢和不喜欢）

这是一个短小的热身活动，目的是让学习者的注意力集中在单元主题上。典型的活动就是学习者读句子，然后根据个人的好恶在表格中进行个性化选择。

🔲 Words and phrases（单词和短语）

这一部分列出了与单元主题相关的 20~30 个关键词和短语。学习者首先浏览这些词语，检查自己是否知道它们的意思，然后通过"Match it"、"Fill it"和"Put it together"三个练习使用这些词语，扩展自己的词汇量。

🗨 Conversation questions（对话问句）

本部分让学习者练习在口语中使用与单元主题相关的常见问句。"Watch out!"提醒学习者在口语中常犯的错误；"Language point"针对出现在本单元的几个口语句型或结构进行精练的讲解；

"PRACTICE" 供学习者进一步理解并练习上一部分出现的句型或结构。

🗨 **Conversation strategies**（对话策略）

这一部分是每个单元的核心，提供了两页的练习，帮助学习者掌握自然、有效的对话策略。学习者通过练习对话样例学习高频表达，从而成功掌握每一个对话策略；然后通过与语伴合作，有目的地进行对话练习。

🗨 **Conversation listening**（对话听力练习）

学习者会听到三四个与单元主题相关的对话，对话中再现前面学到的对话策略和关键词语。本部分有三个步骤的练习：

A First listening 第一次听，理解大意。

B Second listening 第二次听，注意关键细节。

C Noticing the conversation strategies 这一步骤让学习者特别注意说话者使用的对话策略。

🗨 **Get ready!**（做好准备！）

本部分旨在帮助学习者巩固本单元学到的关键词汇、句型和对话策略。学习者有机会在提供的表格中写下相关的词句，组织语言，以准备和语伴进行对话练习。

🗨 **Do it!**（开口说！）

学习者在这一步开口说话，与自己的语伴进行综合对话训练，把学到的内容用到其中。应该鼓励学习者将自己注意到的语伴在会话中用到的有用的词语和表达记录下来，建设自己的口语语料库。

🗨 **Real conversations**（真实的对话）

这一部分让学习者听到与单元主题相关的真实语境下的对话。说话者来自世界各地，他们有的是英语母语者，有的是像我们一样的非英语母语者。听他们不同的发音，鼓励自己说得更好。

🗨 **Thinking about . . .**（思考……）

每单元最后一部分鼓励学习者批判地思考本单元主题涉及的不同方面。这部分活动精心设计，保证即使英语水平较低的学习者也能顺利参与进来。

更多资源：

本书专门网址：www.nicetalkingwithyou.com

本网站为教师和学生提供更多附加的资源。学习者除了可以下载相关音频文件，还可以点击"Global Voices"（全球的声音），听到来自世界各地的人（英语母语者和非英语母语者）用英语围绕单元主题进行的更多讨论。学习者可以通过本网站分享自己对单元主题的想法，与来自世界各地的英语学习者交流学习心得；学习者还可以访问作者的博客，与作者本人进行在线交流。

Contents

Welcome to Nice Talking with You

What's different about *Nice Talking with You*?

Nice Talking with You is different from other books that you may have used before. There are no dialogs to memorize. Instead, this book will help you have **real conversations**: conversations about you and your friends that help you make and keep relationships with other people. This kind of conversation is very common in all languages, because making and keeping relationships with others is the most important function of spoken language.

How will *Nice Talking with You* **help improve your English?**

* You'll review **vocabulary** you have probably learned before, but have probably never used in conversation.

* You'll practice speaking with easy topics, using basic questions, in **timed conversations**.

* You'll learn how to **get ready** for conversations and get practice noticing the English you and your partners use.

* You'll hear a **wide variety of English** – native speakers from around the world, even non-native speakers of English.

* Most of all, you'll master some important phrases and expressions that will make your conversations smoother and more natural. We call these **conversation strategies**.

What is the goal of the unit?

You will speak English using the new conversation strategies you've learned.

What is the goal of the course?

By the end of this book, you'll be able to use all the conversation strategies you've learned naturally and automatically.

Good luck and have fun!

Tom Kenny and *Linda Woo*

How a unit works

Each unit contains a carefully controlled sequence of activities, which build upon each other. The different sections and their functions are shown below.

Likes and dislikes

This is a short, personalized, warm-up activity to focus students' attention on the topic. Typically, students read the statements and check the boxes.

Words and phrases

Between 20 and 30 key words and phrases related to the unit topic are introduced here. Students first get a chance to check if they understand them and then are given focused practice by doing the activities Match it, Fill it in, and Put it together on the following page.

Conversation questions

Commonly used questions related to the topic are introduced and practiced in this section. Watch out! raises students' awareness of common mistakes; the Language point provides a short, one-point Focus on Form; and PRACTICE gives students the opportunity to check their understanding of the Language point.

Conversation strategies

Key conversation strategies that help students manage conversations more effectively are introduced and practiced on these two pages. For each strategy introduced, several high-frequency expressions are highlighted in model conversations. Students are then given a chance to practice these in a controlled manner.

Conversation listening

Students listen to three or four short conversations on the unit topic, which feature the conversation strategies and vocabulary previously introduced. There are three listening stages:

A First listening This provides listening for gist.

B Second listening This focuses students' attention on key details.

C Noticing the conversation strategies This last stage is designed to raise students' awareness of the strategies used by the speakers.

Get ready!

This section serves to consolidate the vocabulary, question patterns, and conversation strategies highlighted in the unit. Students are given a chance to plan for their conversation by writing notes and relevant language in the boxes provided.

Do it!

Students are now ready to put it all together and practice one or more timed conversations with their partners. They are also encouraged to write down expressions and/or words and phrases they notice their partner using.

 ### Real conversations

This section gives students additional listening practice on the topic. These feature unscripted conversations between native and non-native English speakers from around the world, giving students exposure to a variety of English accents.

 ### Thinking about . . .

This last section of the unit encourages students to think critically about aspects of the unit topic. Activities are carefully scaffolded to ensure that even low level students are able to succeed.

More resources

Website www.nicetalkingwithyou.com

Free additional resources for students and teachers can be found on the Website. The complete audio program in MP3 file format is available to download and listen to. Students are also able to listen to Global Voices. These are authentic, unscripted monologues related to the unit topics, spoken by native and non-native speakers of English.

Introductions

Likes and dislikes

Do you like meeting and talking with new people? Read the statements below and put checks (✔) in the boxes.

	Agree	Not sure	Disagree
I like meeting new people.			
I'm nervous with new people because I don't know what to talk about.			
I can't meet new people by myself. I must have a friend with me.			
I make new friends easily.			
I can't start a conversation with someone I don't know.			

 www.nicetalkingwithyou.com
Share your likes and dislikes with other people like you.

Words and phrases

Check the meaning of these words and phrases. Then use them to do the activities on the next page.

area	club	free time	parents	south
be interested in	commute	hobby	part-time job	suburban
born	dislike	like	retired	town
by myself	east	married	rural	urban
children	family	neighborhood	school	west
city	favorite	north	single	work

Match it

Match the word on the left with the meaning on the right. Write the letter on the line. Then check your answers with a partner.

1. _____ commute
2. _____ hobby
3. _____ club
4. _____ neighborhood
5. _____ suburban
6. _____ rural

a) something to do for fun
b) not inside the city, but not out in the country
c) the place around where you live
d) out in the country
e) travel to work or school from home
f) a group to belong to

Fill it in

Use the words and phrases on page 7 to complete the sentences. Then check your answers with a partner.

1. I have a _____ _____ as a waiter. How about you?
2. I'm from a big city, but I was _____ in a small town.
3. I like reading books in my _____ _____.
4. I want to be a translator because I _____ _____ _____ learning foreign languages.
5. I live _____ _____, but sometimes I wish I had a roommate because I get lonely.
6. My family lives in a _____ area. It's really out in the country!
7. My _____ sport is soccer.
8. I commute to _____ by train. It takes me two hours. I have to wake up at 5 a.m.!

Put it together

Draw a line to put the sentences together.

1. My name is Veronica. It's
2. I was born in Australia,
3. My name is Kazutoshi,
4. I'm interested in travel
5. I like TV and watching

and playing the piano.
so please call me Toshi.
sports like soccer and tennis.
nice to meet you.
but I'm from China.

🎧 **02** **Listen to check your answers.**

Conversation questions

What's your name?
Where are you from?
What do you like doing?

Practice asking and answering the questions above with different partners.

Watch out!

Be careful not to make these common mistakes!

✘	✔
I from Japan.	I'm from Japan.
Now, I live Australia.	Now, I live in Australia.
I interested drawing.	I'm interested in drawing.

Practice saying these out loud so you can remember them.

Language point

is ➔ 's
He *is* from Canada. ➔ He*'s* from Canada.

would ➔ 'd
She *would* like to go there. ➔ She*'d* like to go there.

PRACTICE

Match the verbs. Write the sentence number on the line.

1. I*m* from Japan.   *have* _____

2. We*'re* from the same school.   *is*   _____

3. I*ve* been playing piano for a long time. *am*   _____

4. I*'ll* start studying dance soon.   *are* _____

5. It*'s* very interesting to me.   *will* _____

Conversation strategies

Starting a conversation

Here are some natural ways to start your conversations.

> **How's it going?**

> **How are you doing?**

Responses

> **Great!**
> **Good!**
> **Pretty good.**

> **OK.**
> **Not bad.**
> **All right.**

> **Not so good.**

If you answer *Not so good*, **be ready to say why. For example:**

Not so good. I have a cold.
Not so good. I'm sleepy.

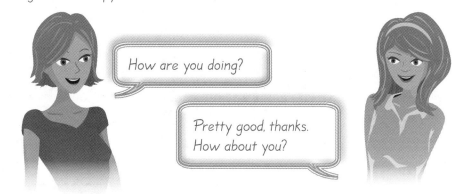

> *How are you doing?*

> *Pretty good, thanks.*
> *How about you?*

PRACTICE

With a partner, ask *How are you doing?* five times. Your partner will use five different answers. Then do the same for *How's it going?*

Ending a conversation

Here's a natural way to end your conversation.

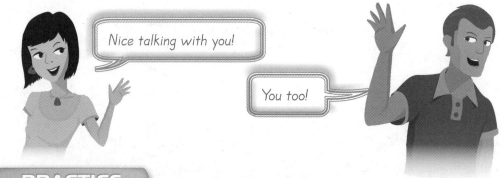

> *Nice talking with you!*

> *You too!*

PRACTICE

Work with a partner. Start conversations again. This time, finish with *Nice talking with you!* and *You too!*

Letting your partner talk

Here is an easy way to ask your partner the same question they ask you.

How about you?

This expression gives your partner a chance to talk.

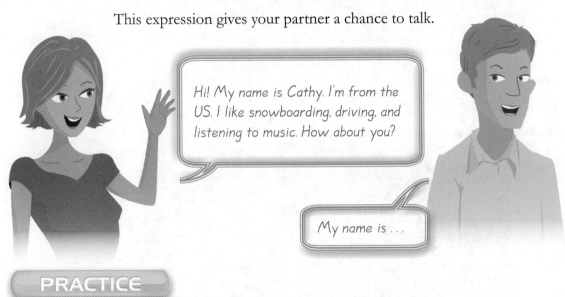

Hi! My name is Cathy. I'm from the US. I like snowboarding, driving, and listening to music. How about you?

My name is . . .

PRACTICE

Use *How about you?* with each partner in your group.

Asking to repeat

Sometimes it's difficult to hear what your partner says. You can use these expressions to ask them to repeat what they said.

Pardon me?   **Excuse me?**

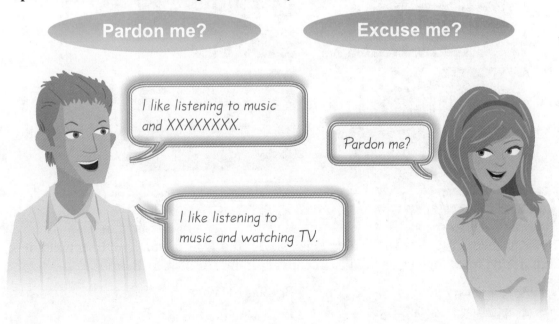

I like listening to music and XXXXXXXX.

Pardon me?

I like listening to music and watching TV.

Conversation listening

03 ▶ A First listening

Where do the speakers live? Number the places in the order you hear about them. One is not used.

a) _____ in the suburbs

b) _____ in a rural area

c) _____ in an apartment with family

d) _____ in the city, downtown

e) _____ in a neighborhood nearby

03 ▶ B Second listening

What are the speakers' hobbies? Circle A or B.

1. A    B

2. A    B

3. A    B

4. A    B

03 ▶ C Noticing the conversation strategies

Some speakers use the expressions *Pardon me?* and *How about you?* Listen again and decide what they refer to in each conversation. Circle A or B.

1. **A** where they live   **B** their hobbies

2. **A** not missing her brother   **B** playing her guitar

3. **A** where he lives   **B** what movies he watches

4. **A** where he lives   **B** if he takes the train

Get ready!

Organize your questions, answers, and vocabulary here to get ready for your *Introductions* conversation.

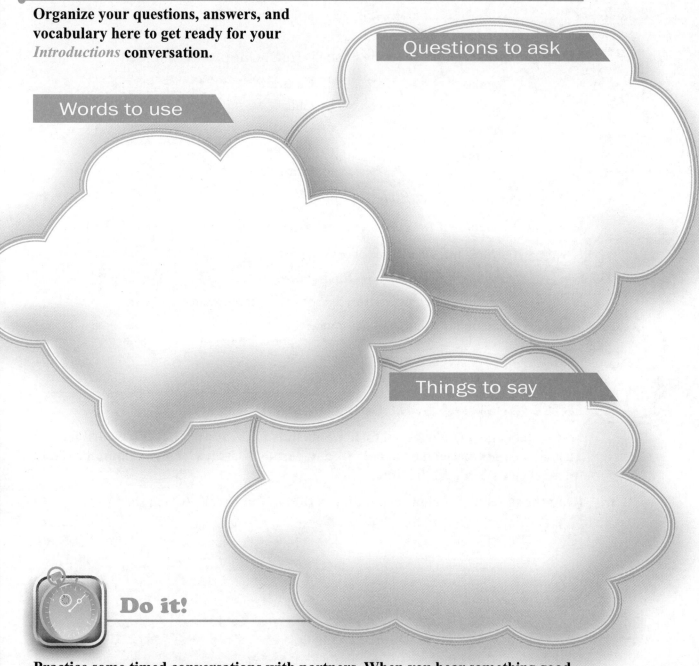

Words to use

Questions to ask

Things to say

Do it!

Practice some timed conversations with partners. When you hear something good, write it on this page after your conversation so you can remember it!

Noticing my partner's English

Real conversations

 A *Listening*

Match the speaker to the place he or she is from. One place is not used.

1. _____ Claudia
2. _____ Sophia
3. _____ William
4. _____ Roxanne

a) Canada
b) Chile
c) Australia
d) England
e) Cambodia

 B *True or false*

Listen again. Decide if the statements are true or false. Write T or F on the lines.

1. _____ Claudia has a tan from outdoor sports.
2. _____ Chihiro lived in the USA for 10 years.
3. _____ William's parents are from Spanish-speaking countries.
4. _____ Roxanne is a designer and a model.

Thinking about . . .

Does meeting new people improve our lives?

Many years ago, people stayed their whole lives in the towns they were born in. They almost never met new people. Today, through fast travel and communications, we meet new people all the time.

Read the statements below. What do you think? Put checks (✔) in the boxes.

	Strongly agree	Agree	Disagree	Strongly disagree
1. It's more dangerous than before to meet new people.				
2. Meeting people from different societies can teach us a lot about the world.				
3. Cultures around the world are becoming the same, so meeting new people isn't so important as before.				
4. Studying English is the key to meeting new people.				

PRACTICE

Share your opinions with your partner. Remember to use the conversation strategies on page 11.

Do you think English is the key to meeting new people?

Yes, I think it's important. How about you?

Yes, me too. But also Chinese and Spanish are very important as well.

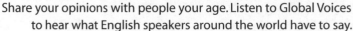

www.nicetalkingwithyou.com

Share your opinions with people your age. Listen to Global Voices to hear what English speakers around the world have to say.

Family

Likes and dislikes

What do you like to do with your family? Put checks (✔) in the boxes below.

I like to . . .

	😃	🙂	😐	🙁	😞
go to restaurants.					
take drives.					
go on picnics.					
go to theme parks.					
play games.					
watch movies.					

www.nicetalkingwithyou.com
Share your likes and dislikes with other people like you.

Words and phrases

Check the meaning of these words and phrases. Then use them to do the activities on the next page.

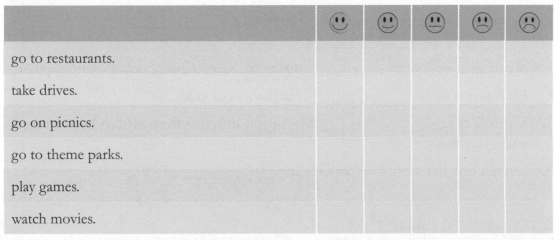

a grandparent	bossy	overweight	talkative
a younger brother	cousin	pass away	tall
an older sister	easygoing	pet	the middle child
an only child	funny	relatives	the oldest
average	get along well	selfish	the youngest
bald	hardworking	short	thin
be different from (someone)	heavy	spoiled	typical
be like (someone)	old	strict	young

Match it

Match the word or phrase on the left with the meaning on the right. Write the letter on the line. Then check your answers with a partner.

1. _____ selfish
2. _____ bossy
3. _____ get along well
4. _____ overweight
5. _____ bald
6. _____ relatives

a) heavy body; fat
b) family members; people connected to you, but not closely
c) without hair on the head
d) someone who thinks only about himself or herself
e) someone who likes to give orders to people, like "Do this" or "Do that"
f) have a good relationship

Fill it in

Use the words and phrases on page 15 to complete the sentences. Then check your answers with a partner.

1. I don't like being _____ _____ _____ because I get lonely sometimes. I wish I had an older sister!

2. My sister _____ _____ my mother. They have the same eyes and nose.

3. I _____ _____ _____ my sister in several ways. For example, I love rock music but she hates it!

4. I have an older sister and a younger brother. I am _____ _____ _____ .

5. My mother is very _____ . Once she starts talking, nobody can stop her.

6. My father is really _____ . He has lots of rules.

7. My sister is very _____ . She's really different from my brother, who gets angry very easily.

8. I have a dog and a cat. Do you have any _____ ?

Put it together

Draw a line to put the sentences together.

1. There are five   not so tall and a little bit fat.
2. I have a   with my mother.
3. My father is   people in my family.
4. I get along well   big family.

 **05** **Listen to check your answers.**

Conversation questions

> How many people are there in your family?
> What's your mother like?
> What does your father look like?

Practice asking and answering the questions above with different partners.

Watch out!

Be careful not to make these common mistakes!

✗	✔
~~My family is five people.~~	There are five people in my family.
~~He looks like tall.~~	He's tall.
~~She's like strict.~~	She's strict.

Practice saying these out loud so you can remember them.

Language point

There is / There's

There is a train station next to my building.

There's a train station next to my building.

There are / There're

There are five people in my family.

There're five people in my family.

PRACTICE

Read the sentences below. Circle *There is* **or** *There are*.

1. *There is / There are* lots of tall buildings in my neighborhood.
2. *There is / There are* a nice park near my house.
3. *There is / There are* some beautiful trees in my backyard.
4. *There is / There are* two pets in my family.
5. *There is / There are* a big window in my bedroom.

Conversation strategies

Repeating

An easy way to react in English is to repeat what your partner says.

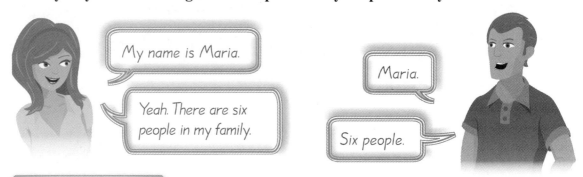

My name is Maria.

Yeah. There are six people in my family.

Maria.

Six people.

PRACTICE

Read the sentences below to the teacher. Your teacher will repeat the key words. Then expressions with a partner.

1. My name is Susan Yang.

2. There are seven people in my family: my mother, father, grandfather, grandmother, me, my older sister, and my younger brother.

3. My mother is very friendly and funny. She's like a friend.

4. My father is handsome, but a little bald.

Getting time to think

When a partner asks you a question, sometimes you can't answer quickly. Use these expressions to get time to think.

Hmm . . . Let me see.
Hmm . . . Let me think.

That's a good question.
That's a difficult question.

Who's the most handsome person in your family?

Hmm . . . Let me see . . . That's a difficult question. Maybe my brother.

You can also repeat the question.

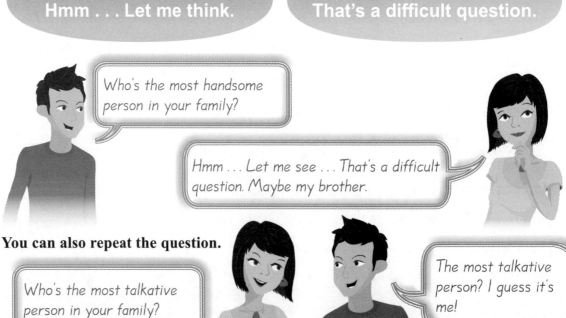

Who's the most talkative person in your family?

The most talkative person? I guess it's me!

Read the questions below. Choose five questions to ask your partner. Write each question on the lines below.

Who do you get along well with in your family?

Who are you like?

Who do you look like?

What's your father's/mother's/sister's/brother's/grandfather's best point?

What's your father's/mother's/sister's/brother's/grandfather's worst point?

Who is the smartest/funniest/loudest person in your family?

Who's the most interesting/talkative/serious person in your family?

What does your mother/father enjoy doing?

What famous person does your brother/sister/father/mother look like?

Who fights the most in your family?

1. _____

2. _____

3. _____

4. _____

5. _____

Now ask your partner the questions. When your partner asks you, use the conversation strategies on page 18 to get time to think.

Conversation listening

 A First listening

Who are the speakers talking about? Number the pictures in the order you hear about them. One is not used.

A Student Award

 B Second listening

What words correctly describe the people? Put checks (✔) in the boxes.

1. ☐ cool ☐ average ☐ tall ☐ handsome
2. ☐ sweet ☐ heavy ☐ quiet ☐ not active
3. ☐ smart ☐ difficult ☐ jealous ☐ hardworking
4. ☐ bald ☐ small eyes ☐ interesting ☐ selfish

 C Noticing the conversation strategies

The expression *That's a(n) . . . question* is used in each conversation. Listen again and match the conversations with the expressions. One is not used.

Expression

a) That's an easy question. _____

b) That's a tough question. _____

c) That's an interesting question. _____

d) That's a difficult question. _____

e) That's a funny question. _____

Get ready!

Organize your questions, answers, and vocabulary here to get ready for your *Family* conversation.

Questions to ask

Words to use

Things to say

Do it!

Practice some timed conversations with partners. When you hear something good, write it on this page after your conversation so you can remember it!

Noticing my partner's English

Real conversations

 A *Listening*

Listen to the conversations about families. Put the questions in the order you hear them.

a) _____ Do you spend much time with your mom?

b) _____ Who do you get along with?

c) _____ What are your parents like?

d) _____ What's your father like?

e) _____ Did you fight a lot when you were younger?

f) _____ What's your mom like?

g) _____ What about your dad?

 B *Vocabulary*

Below are some words or phrases the speakers use. Match them to their meanings.

1. _____ eccentric
2. _____ open person
3. _____ the baby
4. _____ curfew
5. _____ down-to-earth

a) the time by which a child must return home
b) practical, realistic
c) unusual, not the same as others
d) the youngest child in a family
e) someone who likes to experience new things

Thinking about . . .

How important is family?

Different cultures have different attitudes about the importance of family. Read the statements below. Write A if you agree and D if you disagree.

1. _____ Children need both a mother and a father – not just one parent.
2. _____ Children must respect and obey their parents.
3. _____ Parents, not schools, should teach children what is right and what is wrong.
4. _____ Parents should listen to their child's opinion.
5. _____ A couple should never divorce. They should stay together because it is better for the children.

PRACTICE

Share your opinions with your partner. Remember to use the conversation strategies on page 18.

> Do you think a couple should never divorce?

> Divorce? Hmm . . . That's a difficult question. Yes, I guess so. Divorce can be very bad for the children.

> Really? Do you think so? I think sometimes it's OK.

 www.nicetalkingwithyou.com
Share your opinions with people your age. Listen to Global Voices to hear what English speakers around the world have to say.

Shopping

Likes and dislikes

What kind of shopping do you like? Put checks (✔) in the boxes below.

I like shopping for . . .

	😀	🙂	😐	🙁	☹️
clothes and accessories.					
music and movies.					
books and magazines.					
games and software.					
things for my room or home.					

www.nicetalkingwithyou.com
Share your likes and dislikes with other people like you.

Words and phrases

Check the meaning of these words and phrases. Then use them to do the activities on the next page.

advertisements	comparison shopping	go with a friend	price
bargain	consignment shops	good deal	products
brand-name	customer	good quality	retail outlets
cashier	department stores	guarantee	return
cheap	discount	impulse buyer	salesperson
commercials	expensive	low quality	try something on
compare prices	go alone	never miss	window-shopping

Match it

Match the word or phrase on the left with the meaning on the right. Write the letter on the line. Then check your answers with a partner.

1. _____ consignment shops

2. _____ return

3. _____ cashier

4. _____ good deal

5. _____ cheap

6. _____ comparison shopping

a) checking the price of a product at different stores

b) stores where you can buy used goods

c) not expensive – low price

d) the person in a store who works at the register

e) a product you get for a lower price than normal

f) take a product back to the store

Fill it in

Use the words and phrases on page 23 to complete the sentences. Then check your answers with a partner.

1. This game doesn't work. The store has a 30-day _____, so I'm going to return it.

2. Shopping is best when you have money. But if you don't have money, you can always enjoy _____.

3. Famous _____ products are usually expensive, but they're of good quality.

4. Shopping is more fun when you _____ _____ _____ _____.

5. I like to buy clothes in a shop because I can _____ _____ _____ before I buy it, to make sure it fits.

6. Buying things in _____ _____ saves money, but their parking lots are often so big you can't find your car later!

7. The department store is going out of business, so they are selling everything at a 50% _____.

8. I'm an _____ _____ – if I see something I want, I don't think about it. I just buy it.

Put it together

Draw a line to put the sentences together.

1. I like shopping   at all.

2. I don't like shopping   clothes and games and DVDs.

3. I go shopping about   very much.

4. I like shopping for   once a week.

08 **Listen to check your answers.**

Conversation questions

> How much do you like shopping?
> How often do you go shopping?
> What do you like to shop for?

Practice asking and answering the questions above with different partners.

Watch out!

Be careful not to make these common mistakes!

go to shopping

I didn't have money, so I didn't buy.

It takes much money.

go shopping

. . . so I didn't buy anything.

It's expensive.

Practice saying these out loud so you can remember them.

Language point

(not) much/many

If the noun is uncountable, use *much*:

(not) ***much*** — money, cash, stuff

If the noun is countable and plural, use *many*:

(not) ***many*** — bags, dollars, things

Much and *many* are usually used with *not* and in *questions*.

PRACTICE

Circle *much* or *many* to complete the sentences.

1. She didn't spend *much / many* money in the store.

2. My closet is full of so *much / many* shoes.

3. I don't have *much / many* CDs to listen to.

4. How *much / many* rice do you want to eat?

5. I want to have as *much / many* rings as my sister.

Conversation strategies

Showing interest

Oh, really?   Oh, yeah?

Be active when you are listening. Use these expressions to show you are interested in what your partner is saying.

I'm going shopping this weekend.

Oh, yeah? Where?

PRACTICE

Fill in the blanks to complete each sentence below. Then tell each one to your partner. Practice using the expressions above.

1. My favorite thing to buy is _____.

2. I like to go shopping with _____.

3. I don't like to go shopping for _____.

4. I think buying _____ is a waste of money!

5. Recently I bought _____.

6. _____ is probably my favorite department store.

Showing you are listening

Uh-huh.   Mm-hmm.

Use these words to show your partner you are listening. It will help make the conversation go smoothly.

But the thing I like to buy the most . . .

Uh-huh.

. . . is T-shirts! I'm collecting them from around the world.

Oh, really?

PRACTICE

Listen to the passage when your partner reads it. Show you are listening – use one of the expressions on page 26 when you hear a small pause.

"When I was a kid, my parents took me downtown to go shopping almost every weekend. ‖ Of course, I was always happy when they bought me something, ‖ but even if we didn't have much money it was always interesting to see what was new. ‖ For us, shopping is kind of entertainment; ‖ it's a way to have fun with the family. ‖ Now that I'm older, ‖ it's great to have my own money. ‖ It feels good to buy something with money I made myself, ‖ not money just from my parents."

Now read the passage to your partner and practice using the expressions.

Introducing a question

So, . . .

You can use *So* to introduce a question into your conversation.

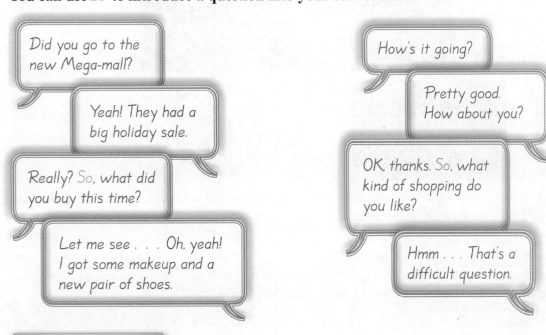

Did you go to the new Mega-mall?

Yeah! They had a big holiday sale.

Really? So, what did you buy this time?

Let me see . . . Oh, yeah! I got some makeup and a new pair of shoes.

How's it going?

Pretty good. How about you?

OK, thanks. So, what kind of shopping do you like?

Hmm . . . That's a difficult question.

PRACTICE

Ask and answer the shopping conversation questions with a partner again. This time, use *So* to introduce a question.

Conversation listening

 A First listening

Where do the speakers decide to shop at? Circle A or B.

1. **A** Department store   **B** Consignment store
2. **A** Famous brand clothing store   **B** Casual clothing store
3. **A** Furniture store   **B** Electronics store
4. **A** Department store   **B** Shopping mall

 B Second listening

What are the speakers going to buy? Circle A or B.

1. **A**    **B**

2. **A**    **B**

3. **A**    **B**

4. **A**    **B**

 C Noticing the conversation strategies

In each conversation, one person uses the expressions *Uh-huh*, *Mm-hmm*, *Yeah?* or *Really?* to react to what their partner says. Who reacts more in each conversation, the man or the woman? Put checks (✔) in the boxes.

	Man	Woman		Man	Woman
1.	☐	☐	3.	☐	☐
2.	☐	☐	4.	☐	☐

Get ready!

Organize your questions, answers, and vocabulary here to get ready for your *Shopping* conversation.

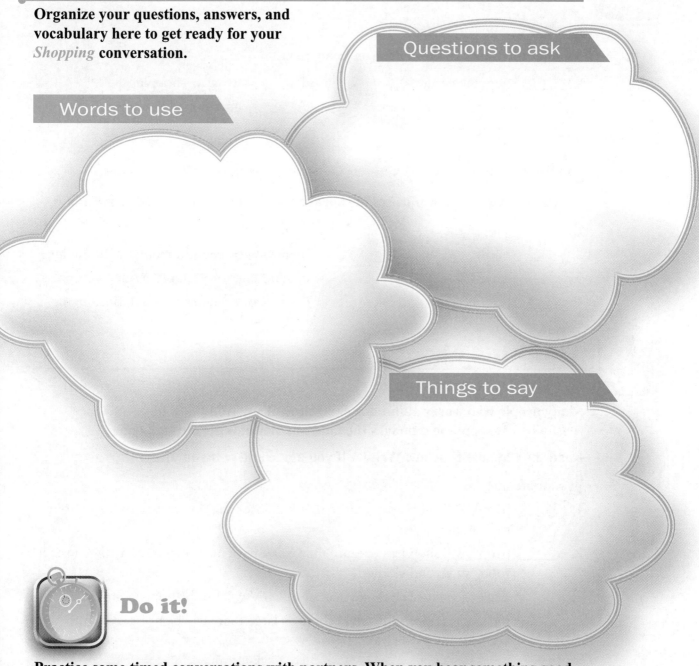

Questions to ask

Words to use

Things to say

Do it!

Practice some timed conversations with partners. When you hear something good, write it on this page after your conversation so you can remember it!

Noticing my partner's English

....

....

....

....

....

Real conversations

 A Listening

Number the topics in the order you hear them.

a) _____ shopping online   d) _____ window-shopping

b) _____ how to pay for items   e) _____ guys don't like shopping

c) _____ buying shoes

10 B Vocabulary

Here are some words or phrases the speakers use. Match them to their meanings.

1. _____ shopaholic   a) really like

2. _____ outfit   b) buying on the Internet without thinking

3. _____ crazy about   c) clothing, for example, a one-piece dress

4. _____ just one click   d) someone who is addicted to shopping

 Thinking about . . .

Should we buy less?

Many people who worry about our environment say we should buy less. One reason is that shopping damages the land and pollutes the air and water.

Read the statements below. Write A if you agree and D if you disagree.

In your lifetime . . .

1. _____ people will shop less because they will lose the good feeling they get from buying things.

2. _____ people will shop less because they won't have money to buy anything except food, water, and clothes.

3. _____ advertisements will disappear because TV will not be popular anymore.

4. _____ the world population will become so large there will be no space left to keep the things we buy.

5. _____ consuming will continue, and no one will be able to stop it.

 PRACTICE

Share your opinions with your partner. Remember to use the conversation strategies on pages 26 and 27.

> Do you think people will shop less in the future?

> Maybe. Shopping isn't so good for the environment. What do you think?

> I think that shopping makes people happy, so shopping will always continue.

> Oh, really?

www.nicetalkingwithyou.com

Share your opinions with people your age. Listen to Global Voices to hear what English speakers around the world have to say.

Unit 4

Food

Likes and dislikes

What do you like to eat? Put checks (✔) in the boxes below.

I like to eat . . .

	☺	🙂	😐	🙁	☹			☺	🙂	😐	🙁	☹
beef							mangoes					
bread							noodles					
chicken							pizza					
curry							pork					
fish							rice					
grapefruit							shrimp					
lemon pie							squid					
lobster							vegetables					

www.nicetalkingwithyou.com
Share your likes and dislikes with other people like you.

Words and phrases

Check the meaning of these words and phrases. Then use them to do the activities on the next page.

allergic to	fish	healthy	quick and easy	tastes terrible
bad for you	fresh	junk food	raw	too many
bitter	fried	leftovers	seafood	calories
delicious	fruit	light	snack	vegetables
desserts	go out to eat	on a diet	spicy	vegetarian
fast food	good for you	pack a lunch	sweets	yummy
fattening	greasy	portions	tastes great	

Match it

Match the word or phrase on the left with the meaning on the right. Write the letter on the line. Then check your answers with a partner.

1. _____ greasy

2. _____ bitter

3. _____ junk food

4. _____ allergic to

5. _____ raw

6. _____ nutritious

a) not cooked, for example, uncooked fish

b) unable to eat or touch something because it gives you a bad reaction

c) food or drink that helps keep you healthy

d) a kind of taste, for example, black coffee

e) cooked with a lot of oil

f) food that is not healthy and often has many calories

Fill it in

Use the words and phrases on page 31 to complete the sentences. Then check your answers with a partner.

1. Tofu is really _____ _____ _____ because it has a lot of protein and it doesn't have _____ _____ _____.

2. I don't have time to cook, so I usually _____ _____ _____ _____.

3. I often have a _____ in the afternoon, usually something sweet.

4. The _____ at restaurants are so large that I usually can't finish everything.

5. Mapo Tofu is too _____. I can't eat it.

6. I often double a recipe when I make something, but then I have to eat _____ for several days!

7. If you're _____ _____ _____, you shouldn't eat _____ _____ like hamburgers or fries.

8. The meal she cooked tonight was _____! I think she's a great cook.

Put it together

Draw a line to put the sentences together.

1. I like many   every day.

2. I like it   it because it tastes bitter.

3. I eat it almost   kinds of food.

4. I don't like   because it's sweet.

11 **Listen to check your answers.**

Conversation questions

> What food do you like?
> What kind of ice cream do you like?
> Is there any food you don't like?

Practice asking and answering the questions above with different partners.

Watch out!

Be careful not to make these common mistakes!

✘	✔
Pizza is good taste.	Pizza tastes good.
Tofu is good for health.	Tofu is good for you / your health.
I don't eat yet.	I've never eaten it before.

Practice saying these out loud so you can remember them.

Language point

Why?

A: I eat six apples a day.

B: *Why?*

Why not?

A: I don't like ice cream.

B: *Why not?*

PRACTICE

Look at the words below and decide which response to use. Put checks (✔) in the boxes.

		Why?	Why not?
1.	I can't eat liver.	☐	☐
2.	I don't like chocolate snacks.	☐	☐
3.	I have to eat rice at every meal.	☐	☐
4.	I never eat fast food.	☐	☐
5.	I like soda more than tea.	☐	☐

Conversation strategies

Agreeing and disagreeing
① positive statements

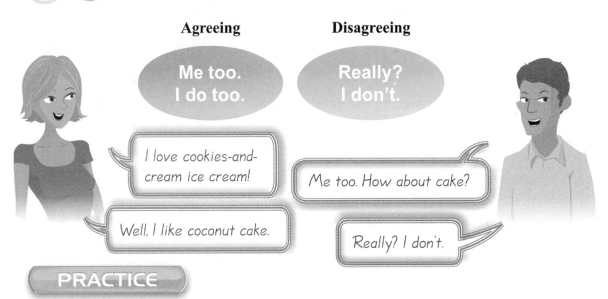

Agreeing

Me too.
I do too.

Disagreeing

Really?
I don't.

I love cookies-and-cream ice cream!

Me too. How about cake?

Well, I like coconut cake.

Really? I don't.

PRACTICE

Write five things that you like to eat. Then tell your partner. Your partner will use an expression to agree or disagree.

I like . . .

1. _____
2. _____
3. _____
4. _____
5. _____

Agreeing and disagreeing
② negative statements

Agreeing

Me neither.
I don't either.

Disagreeing

Really? I do.

I really don't like liver!

Me neither. What else don't you like?

Um, I don't like celery.

Really? I do.

PRACTICE

Write three things that you don't like to eat and two things that you like to eat.
Then tell your partner. Your partner will use an expression to agree or disagree.

I like / don't like . . .

1. _____
2. _____
3. _____
4. _____
5. _____

Your partner	You	
	Agree	Disagree
I like . . .	Me too. I do too.	Really? I don't.
I don't like . . .	Me neither. I don't either.	Really? I do.

Asking for more information

To keep the conversation going, you can use this expression.

What else?

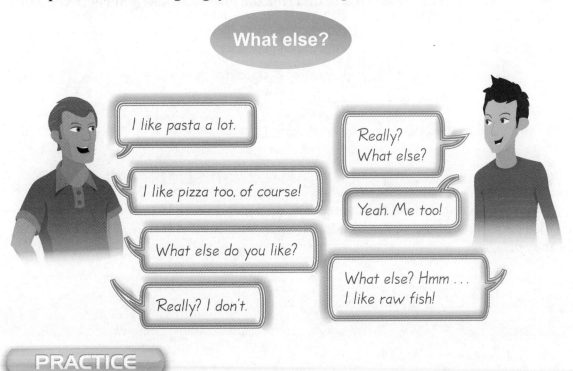

I like pasta a lot.

Really?
What else?

I like pizza too, of course!

Yeah. Me too!

What else do you like?

What else? Hmm . . .
I like raw fish!

Really? I don't.

PRACTICE

Use your list of foods on page 31 to practice agreeing and disagreeing again. This
time, use *What else?* to extend your conversation.

A First listening

What foods or drinks are the speakers talking about? Number the pictures in the order you hear about them. One is not used.

B Second listening

What words do the speakers use to describe the food or drink? Put checks (✔) in the boxes.

1. coffee ☐ bitter ☐ sugary
2. chili peppers ☐ spicy ☐ healthy
3. lettuce ☐ crunchy ☐ crisp
4. home-style cooking ☐ fast ☐ healthy

C Noticing the conversation strategies

The speakers use some of the expressions on pages 34 and 35 to agree or disagree with each other about certain foods. Listen again. Circle A if they agree and D if they disagree.

1. coffee A / D
2. tea A / D
3. pasta A / D
4. chili peppers A / D
5. carrots A / D
6. cabbage A / D
7. rice, fish, and vegetables A / D

Get ready!

Organize your questions, answers, and vocabulary here to get ready for your *Food* conversation.

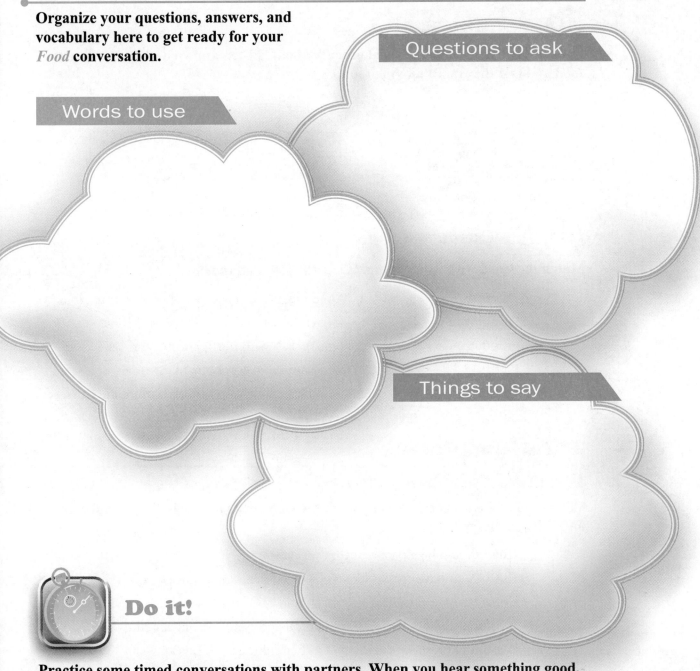

Questions to ask

Words to use

Things to say

Do it!

Practice some timed conversations with partners. When you hear something good, write it on this page after your conversation so you can remember it!

Noticing my partner's English

Real conversations

 ## A *Listening*

Look at the list of foods the speakers talk about. Listen and write L if they like the food and D if they don't like the food.

_____ seafood   _____ junk food

_____ pasta   _____ Thai food

_____ vegetables   _____ mushrooms

_____ fast food   _____ cucumbers

_____ meat and potatoes   _____ tomatoes

B *Vocabulary*

Match the word with its meaning. Write the letter on the line.

1. _____ lasagna   a) something that looks, tastes, or smells terrible
2. _____ nagging   b) soft; not crisp
3. _____ fondue   c) a pasta dish with meat, cheese, and sauce
4. _____ gross   d) complaining to someone many times
5. _____ mushy   e) food dipped into a pot filled with melted cheese

Thinking about . . .

Food, health, and culture

What kind of food is good for you? Read the statements below. Write A if you agree and D if you disagree.

1. _____ Rice should be a part of every meal.
2. _____ It's OK to have snacks like chips or cookies sometimes.
3. _____ Meat isn't very healthy. People should eat more vegetables instead.
4. _____ Cultural changes in a diet are natural and cannot be changed.
5. _____ We should respect the diets of other cultures.
6. _____ What we decide to eat and drink affects the environment.

 PRACTICE

Share your opinions with your partner. Remember to use the conversation strategies on pages 34 and 35.

> Do you think that meat is unhealthy?

> I think it's probably OK sometimes.

> Me too. Eating vegetables is better for the environment, but I think a little meat is OK.

www.nicetalkingwithyou.com

Share your opinions with people your age. Listen to Global Voices to hear what English speakers around the world have to say.

Music

Likes and dislikes

What music do you like?

Put checks (✔) next to the genres you like and crosses (✗) next to the genres you don't like.

I listen to . . .

pop	☐	jazz	☐
rock	☐	traditional	☐
R&B	☐	classic rock	☐
classical	☐	rap/hip-hop	☐
punk	☐		

www.nicetalkingwithyou.com
Share your likes and dislikes with other people like you.

Words and phrases

Check the meaning of these words and phrases. Then use them to do the activities on the next page.

background vocals	find out about	lyrics	recommend	smooth
ballad	harmony	melody	relaxing	soft
band	heavy metal	moving	rhythm	sold-out
composer	impressive	musical instrument	salsa	songwriter
download	live concert	performance	singer	soothing
	loud		slow	soundtrack

Match it

Match the word on the left with the meaning on the right. Write the letter on the line. Then check your answers with a partner.

1. _____ moving
2. _____ composer
3. _____ sold-out
4. _____ download
5. _____ lyrics
6. _____ impressive

a) get something from the Internet

b) when all tickets to an event have been bought

c) the words to a song

d) something you admire and think is very good

e) a person who writes music

f) cause to have strong feelings, such as sadness or sympathy

Fill it in

Use the words and phrases on page 39 to complete the sentences. Then check your answers with a partner.

1. Can you turn down the volume, please? The music is too _____.

2. I think that he is much better as a songwriter than a _____. His voice just doesn't sound very good.

3. The movie was just OK, but the music from the _____ was impressive.

4. My sister plays piano, but I can't play any _____ _____.

5. I love going to a _____ _____. It's more exciting than just listening to CDs.

6. My brother likes heavy metal and rock music, but I like more _____ and relaxing music.

7. My favorite kind of music is salsa. The upbeat _____ and background vocals are so much fun to listen to and dance to.

8. How do I _____ _____ _____ new music? I read recommendations on the Internet and _____ songs. Or my friends and I exchange CDs.

Put it together

Draw a line to put the sentences together.

1. I love hip-hop

2. I practice guitar

3. I listen to

4. I don't like classical

music – I think it's boring.

Beyoncé – I have all her music.

and I like playing rock music.

music – it's great to dance to.

14 **Listen to check your answers.**

Conversation questions

> What kind of music do you like?
> Who's your favorite group/singer?
> Who/What don't you like?

Practice asking and answering the questions above with different partners.

Watch out!

Be careful not to make these common mistakes!

✗	✔
~~When I listen her, I am exciting.~~	When I listen to her, I get excited.
~~I know only his name.~~	I've heard of him, but I've never listened to him.
~~I want to go to their live.~~	I want to go to their concert.

Practice saying these out loud so you can remember them.

Language point

him   her   them   it

I like Chopstick Brothers. Do you know *them*?

I love Jay Chou. Do you know *him*?

I think " Way to Your Heart " is great. Have you heard *it*?

PRACTICE

Fill in the boxes below with names of your favorite singers or groups and songs. Then ask if your partner knows that song, singer, or group. Use *him*, *her*, *them*, or *it*.

Group	Male singer	Female singer	Song

Conversation strategies

Asking for examples

Sometimes your partner will say something interesting and you want to know more. When you ask for examples, use these expressions to ask for more information.

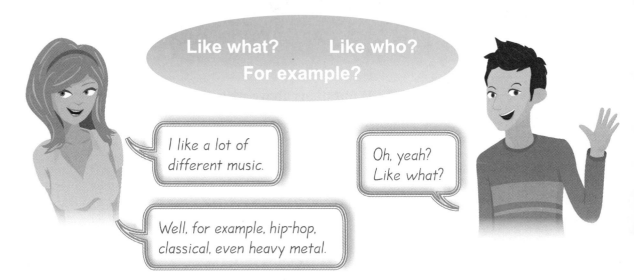

Like what?   Like who?
For example?

I like a lot of different music.

Oh, yeah? Like what?

Well, for example, hip-hop, classical, even heavy metal.

PRACTICE

Read the statements about music below. Choose six that you like and put a check (✔) next to them. Then write an example for each statement.

✔	Statement	Your example
	I like different kinds of music.	
	I like lots of different groups.	
	I like songs by . . .	
	I like songs that cheer me up.	
	I like music that relaxes me.	
	I don't like listening to loud music.	
	When I go driving, I listen to my favorite songs.	
	I don't like some of the songs on the radio these days.	
	I don't like the music my father listens to in the car.	

Now compare with a partner. Remember to use the expressions above.

Tripling your reaction

You can show your excitement in English by repeating a word or phrase. When you repeat it three times, this is called tripling.

I really like Black-Eyed Peas.

Me too! Me too! Me too!

Do you know their song, "Where Is the Love"?

Yeah! Yeah! Yeah!

You can also use different words and phrases.

You know Green Day, right?

Sure, sure, of course!

PRACTICE

Make your own list of triples by combining some of these common expressions.

Absolutely. Yes. Yeah. Right. Exactly.

All the time. Great. Of course. No. Sure.

My triples

1. _____ _____ _____

2. _____ _____ _____

Share your triples with the class. Then practice them in a conversation about music with a partner.

A First listening

What are the speakers doing? Number the pictures in the order you hear about them. One is not used.

 B Second listening

Why do the speakers like the music they talk about? Match the types of music with the reasons they give.

Types of music	Reasons
Ballads	
Classic rock	lets me be creative
Classical	relaxing
Dance music	cheers you up
Pop	gives me energy
Punk and metal	
Rap	

 C Noticing the conversation strategies

The speakers use the expressions *Like who?*, *Like what?*, **and** *For example?*. **What do the expressions refer to? Circle A or B.**

1. **A** the kind of ballads she likes **B** the kind of rap she doesn't like
2. **A** new ways to dance **B** new music videos
3. **A** other kinds of music he listens to **B** other songs he likes
4. **A** an example of a Website **B** an example of an instrument

Get ready!

Organize your questions, answers, and vocabulary here to get ready for your *Music* conversation.

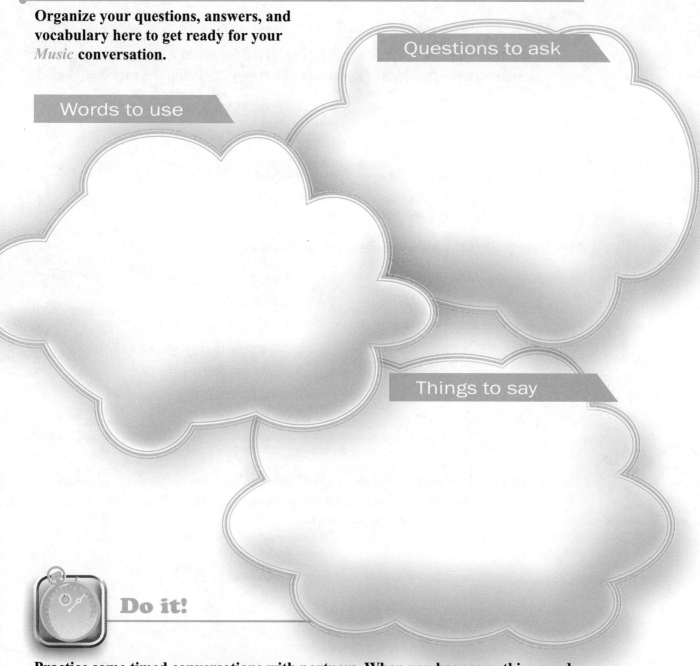

Words to use

Questions to ask

Things to say

Do it!

Practice some timed conversations with partners. When you hear something good, write it on this page after your conversation so you can remember it!

Noticing my partner's English

Real conversations

 A **Listening**

Look at the list of music types. Listen to the conversations and decide if the speakers mostly like or don't like the kinds of music. Write **L** if they like it and **D** if they don't like it.

_____	R&B and hip-hop	_____	K-Pop
_____	house	_____	classical
_____	Japanese visual music	_____	rock
_____	British indie music	_____	rap

16 **B** **Vocabulary**

Match the part of the phrase in _italics_ with its meaning.

1. _____ _it's all about the beat_   a) having fun
2. _____ when you're _partying_   b) difficult to understand
3. _____ clothes are very _flashy_   c) try to understand
4. _____ video is very _complex_   d) the music is most important
5. _____ _analyze the meanings_   e) bright and expensive

Thinking about . . .

Music

"No music, no life" is a common saying. It's hard to imagine a life without music. Why is music so important to us? Read the statements below. Number the reasons. (**1** = most important; **5** = least important)

Music . . .

1. _____ gives us a chance to become rich and famous.
2. _____ lets us be creative.
3. _____ helps us enjoy our lives.
4. _____ is social – it draws people together.
5. _____ is easy – anyone can sing/dance/play to it.

PRACTICE

Share your opinions with your partner. Remember to use the conversation strategies on pages 42 and 43.

> I think music helps us enjoy our lives.

> Really? For example?

> For example, if we're sad or lonely, music can cheer us up. Don't you think so?

> Yeah, yeah, yeah! You're right!

www.nicetalkingwithyou.com
Share your opinions with people your age. Listen to Global Voices to hear what English speakers around the world have to say.

Free time

Likes and dislikes

What do you like to do in your free time? Put the activities below in order.
(1 = you like the most; 6 = you like the least)

Shopping _____   Listening to music _____

Reading _____   Watching TV/movies _____

Meeting new people _____   Doing something outdoors _____

www.nicetalkingwithyou.com
Share your likes and dislikes with other people like you.

Words and phrases

Check the meaning of these words and phrases. Then use them to do the activities on the next page.

challenging	makes me feel good	studying English
collecting	makes me happy	surfing the Internet
cooking	meeting new people	taking classes
dancing	playing games	taking naps
drawing pictures	playing sports	taking photos
driving	playing with my pet	taking weekend trips
fun	reading books	volunteering
get rid of stress	relaxing at home	watching movies
going to restaurants	satisfying	watching TV
listening to music	singing karaoke	writing e-mails

Match it

Match the word or phrase on the left with the meaning on the right. Write the letter on the line. Then check your answers with a partner.

1. _____ taking naps
2. _____ collecting
3. _____ surfing the Internet
4. _____ satisfying
5. _____ volunteering
6. _____ taking classes

a) browsing Websites
b) studying something
c) helping other people
d) keeping a series of something (cards, magazines, etc.)
e) sleeping for a short time
f) giving you a good feeling

Fill it in

Use the words and phrases on page 47 to complete the sentences. Then check your answers with a partner.

1. I enjoy _____ _____ _____ anytime. It's a great chance to make new friends.

2. I like _____ _____, especially novels and mysteries.

3. _____ _____ _____ is fun, but it's cheaper to buy something to eat at a convenience store.

4. I've got a computer at home, so when I'm bored I like _____ _____ _____.

5. _____ _____ _____ to resort areas in the mountains or near the ocean is a nice way to relax with my family.

6. _____ _____ with a good camera is easy and fun.

7. When I get a day off, I usually don't want to go out. I'm happy just _____ _____ _____.

8. I started taking yoga. It's great – you get fit and it helps you _____ _____ _____ _____.

Put it together

Draw a line to put the sentences together.

1. In my free time I   bungee jumping.
2. I don't have a hobby   used to collect sports cards.
3. When I was young, I   these days.
4. No, I've never tried   like reading books.

🎧 **17** **Listen to check your answers.**

Conversation questions

> What do you do in your free time?
> Do you have any hobbies?
> Have you ever . . . ?

Practice asking and answering the questions above with different partners.

Watch out!

Be careful not to make these common mistakes!

✗	✔
It needs much time.	It takes (a lot of) time.
I have ever tried bowling.	I've tried bowling.
I can't drawing pictures.	I can't draw pictures.

Practice saying these out loud so you can remember them.

Language point

Verb	Verb + -ing
He can't **swim**.	I'm good at **swimming**.
She likes to **dance**.	They enjoy **dancing**.
It's good to **read** books.	**Reading** books is **relaxing**.

PRACTICE

Read the sentences below. Circle the correct form of the verb.

1. I like to *play* / *playing* board games, like chess.

2. *Watch* / *Watching* TV is a good way to relax.

3. I don't have time to *do* / *doing* any hobbies.

4. I enjoy *make* / *making* cakes for my family.

5. It's fun to *use* / *using* the Internet.

Conversation strategies

Giving just enough information

In casual conversation, people don't give all the information they could. Use the expressions below when you think your partner understands you enough.

. . . and stuff.

. . . and stuff like that.

> What do you do in your free time?

> Well, at home, I usually watch TV, listen to music, and stuff like that.

> What do you do on the weekends?

> I usually hang out with friends. We go shopping, chat, and stuff.

PRACTICE

What do you like to do in your free time? Look at the chart below. Think of activities you enjoy and complete the chart.

Time/Place		Activity 1		Activity 2
At home,				
At school,				
Downtown,	I like to		and	
On vacation,				
On the weekends,				

Now tell your partner what you like to do. Be sure to use the expressions above.

Being general

In conversation, speakers don't ask questions using long lists. The expression below is often used to make a shorter question and sound polite.

. . . or something?

In your free time, do you ever take a weekend trip or something?

Yeah, I do. My friend has a cabin in the mountains. It's really a great place to go.

On the weekends, do you usually watch movies or something?

Yeah, I love watching horror movies.

PRACTICE

Look at the situations below. Write a question for each one using *or something*.

A trip to Disneyland

Question: _____?

A visit to your grandparents' house

Question: _____?

Some recent downtown shopping

Question: _____?

A recent meal out with friends

Question: _____?

Now ask your partner the questions.

A First listening

What do the speakers do in their free time? What activities do they talk about the most? Circle A or B.

1. A  B

2. A  B

3. A  B

4. A  B

 B Second listening

How long have the speakers been doing these activities? Circle A, B, or C.

1. **A** many years   **B** a few months   **C** just started
2. **A** two years   **B** a few months   **C** just started
3. **A** a few years   **B** a few months   **C** just started
4. **A** a year   **B** a few months   **C** just started

 C Noticing the conversation strategies

The speakers use the expressions *and stuff*, *and stuff like that*, **and** *or something*.
Listen again and decide what these expressions refer to. Circle A or B.

1. **A** things to do in your bedroom   **B** the kinds of comic books you read
2. **A** activity to help people   **B** getting people interested in something
3. **A** starting a band   **B** fun things to do with friends
4. **A** activities to do with friends   **B** activities to lose weight

Get ready!

Organize your questions, answers, and vocabulary here to get ready for your *Free time* **conversation.**

Questions to ask

Words to use

Things to say

Do it!

Practice some timed conversations with partners. When you hear something good, write it on this page after your conversation so you can remember it!

Noticing my partner's English

Real conversations

19 A Listening

Listening to the speakers talk about leisure activities. Number the activities in the order you hear about them.

_____ belly dancing _____ eating cakes _____ skateboarding
_____ bungee-jumping _____ hanging out with friends _____ skydiving
_____ cooking   _____ Internet surfing _____ swimming
_____ designing fashion _____ photography   _____ walking
_____ drinking coffee _____ reading

19 B Vocabulary

Match the phrase with its meaning. Write the letter on the line.

1. _____ put a lot of energy into   a) a display of something
2. _____ for the pleasure of it   b) someone who loves reading
3. _____ an exhibition   c) not busy
4. _____ a bookworm   d) afraid of high places
5. _____ have time to kill   e) for the enjoyment of something
6. _____ scared of heights   f) work very hard on

Thinking about . . .

How important is free time?

What is free time for? How should we spend our free time? How important is it in your society? Look at the list of activities below. How important is each one to you? Put checks (✔) in the boxes.

Activities	Very important	Important	Not important
Resting the body			
Exercising the body			
Doing things to improve the mind			
Relaxing the mind			
Building social relationships			
Scheduling activities and keeping busy			

PRACTICE

Share your opinions with your partner. Remember to use the conversation strategies on pages 50 and 51.

> I think our society keeps us too busy doing group activities and stuff in our free time.

> I think so too. We should just rest and relax!

www.nicetalkingwithyou.com

Share your opinions with people your age. Listen to Global Voices
to hear what English speakers around the world have to say.

Review 1

Conversation strategies

Unit 1

How's it going? / How are you doing?
Great! / Good! / Pretty good.
OK. / Not bad. / All right.
Not so good.
Nice talking with you!
How about you?
Pardon me? / Excuse me?

Unit 2

Hmm . . . Let me see.
Hmm . . . Let me think.
That's a good/difficult question.

Unit 3

Oh, really?
Oh, yeah?
Uh-huh.
Mm-hmm.
So, . . .

Unit 4

Me too.
I do too.
Me neither.
I don't either.
Really? I don't.
Really? I do.
What else?

Unit 5

Like what?
Like who?
For example?
Tripling your reaction

Unit 6

. . . and stuff.
. . . and stuff like that.
. . . or something?

A. Listen to your partner read the sentences below. Each time he or she pauses, respond with one of the expressions below.

> **Oh, yeah?**

> **Really?**

> **Uh-huh.**

> **Mm-hmm.**

Family

I really like my brother. ‖ He's three years older than me. ‖ He's funny ‖ but he can be serious too. ‖ He's like a good friend. ‖ Some people say we are like good friends ‖ and not like brothers. ‖ He talks to me about lots of things. ‖ We talk about school, cars, our friends, and many other things. ‖ I really respect him.

Shopping

I don't have so much money, ‖ so I go window-shopping more than real shopping. If I have money, ‖ I usually buy something fun for myself. For example, I might buy clothes, ‖ or some music, ‖ or a magazine. Shopping is kind of like entertainment, isn't it? ‖ There's a lot to see ‖ if you go to the right places.

B. Write sentences of your own for the two topics below. Then read them to your partner. Your partner will use the expressions above to react.

Food

Music

LISTENING PRACTICE 1

You will hear three conversations. In each conversation the speakers use conversation strategies to help manage the conversation smoothly:

a) In one conversation a speaker works hard to keep the conversation going.

b) In one conversation a speaker gets the other speaker to repeat something.

c) In one conversation a speaker needs some time to answer.

20 Listen to each conversation. Match the descriptions above with the conversation. Write a, b and c on the correct lines below.

Conversation 1 _____   Conversation 2 _____   Conversation 3 _____

SPEAKING PRACTICE 2

You have already learned how to ask for examples and keep the conversation going.

Asking for examples	Keeping the conversation going
Like who/what/where/how?	Who? What? Where/What else?

Example:

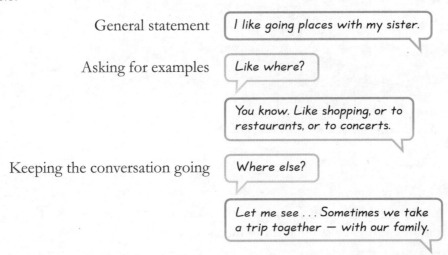

General statement — I like going places with my sister.

Asking for examples — Like where?

You know. Like shopping, or to restaurants, or to concerts.

Keeping the conversation going — Where else?

Let me see ... Sometimes we take a trip together — with our family.

Write a general statement about each topic. Then, with a partner, practice asking for examples and keeping the conversation going.

Topic	General Statement
Family	I like going places with my sister.
Music	
Shopping	
Food	
Free time	

A. In the following two conversations you will hear the speakers use different conversation strategies. Some of the expressions they use are written down below. Listen and write other expressions you hear.

Conversation 1	Conversation 2
How's it going?	So, . . .
Pretty good.	Let me see.

 B. Listen again. In which conversation do the speakers use the strategies below? Put checks (✔) in the boxes.

Strategy	Conversation 1	Conversation 2
Getting time to think		
Asking for examples		
Agreeing		

Travel

Likes and dislikes

What do you enjoy about travel? Put checks (✔) in the boxes below.

I like . . .

	☺	☺	☺	☹	☹
taking photos.					
meeting people.					
using a new language.					
eating local food.					
taking trains.					
flying on airplanes.					
visiting famous places.					
buying souvenirs.					

 www.nicetalkingwithyou.com
Share your likes and dislikes with other people like you.

Words and phrases

Check the meaning of these words and phrases. Then use them to do the activities on the next page.

afraid of flying	customs	jet lag	polluted	sightseeing
airfare	dangerous	lively	popular tourist	souvenir
at a hotel	duty-free store	nice view	destination	tight budget
beach	famous	on a package tour	rates	two nights and
breakfast buffet	guidebook	on a trip	reservation	three days
busy	humid	peaceful	safe	
crowded	immigration	plan a trip	scenery	

Match it

Match the word or phrase on the left with the meaning on the right. Write the letter on the line. Then check your answers with a partner.

1. _____ duty-free store
2. _____ reservation
3. _____ customs
4. _____ immigration
5. _____ famous
6. _____ jet lag

a) the place where people check your passport when you enter a country
b) stores which sell goods with no tax
c) feeling tired after flying because of the time difference
d) something or someone that everyone knows
e) the place where people check your bags when you enter a country
f) a guarantee that you have a hotel room, a seat on a plane, train, etc.

Fill it in

Use the words and phrases on page 59 to complete the sentences. Then check your answers with a partner.

1. I don't like to travel _____ _____ _____ _____. I like to plan things by myself.

2. We went sightseeing to the _____ _____ _____ in the area. It was interesting but crowded with other tourists.

3. I don't like to buy many _____ to bring back to my friends. I don't have so much money!

4. We arrived on Thursday afternoon, and we left the hotel on Saturday evening. It was just for _____ _____ _____ _____ _____.

5. Every morning, the hotel has a wonderful _____ _____.

6. The island is known for its beautiful sandy _____.

7. We had a _____ _____ from our hotel window. We could see the whole city.

8. If you wait to fly in the fall or winter, you will be able to find cheaper _____.

Put it together

Draw a line to complete the sentences.

1. I have traveled abroad
2. I haven't been to Europe
3. Australia was a really
4. It was my first time

great place to visit.
to go on an airplane.
only one time, to Canada.
yet, but I want to go.

 **22** Listen to check your answers.

Conversation questions

> Where have you traveled?
> How did you get there?
> What did you do there?
> How was it?

Practice asking and answering the questions above with different partners.

Watch out!

Be careful not to make these common mistakes!

✗

~~I went to abroad.~~

~~I went America for homestay.~~

~~I could enjoy.~~

✔

I went abroad.

I went to America for a homestay.

I enjoyed it. / I had fun.

Practice saying these out loud so you can remember them.

Language point

be → has/have been	I've *(have)* *been* to China.
see → has/have seen	She's *(has)* *seen* the Eiffel Tower.
climb → has/have climbed	She's *(has)* *climbed* Mt. Fuji.

Choose the verb from the box and write the correct form on the lines below.

eat   fly   hold   travel   try

1. Have you _____ by ship before?

2. I have never _____ sushi.

3. I've _____ a koala before.

4. I've never _____ in first class.

5. Have you ever _____ the fruit durian?

Conversation strategies

Showing surprise

When your partner says something exciting, use these common expressions.

> You're kidding!
> Oh my gosh!

> You're lucky!
> I'm so jealous!

I took a photo from the top of the Eiffel Tower!

Wow! I'm so jealous!

PRACTICE

Work with a partner. One is Student A; the other is Student B. Read the sentences below to your partner. Your partner will use one of the expressions above to react.

Student A	Student B
1. Last year I went to Hawaii twice!	1. I've been to Europe five times.
2. I always fly in first class.	2. I always stay in the most expensive hotel.
3. I've traveled to 15 countries.	3. I held a real koala in Australia.
4. I got an extra two free nights at my hotel.	4. I travel abroad almost every week.

Reacting to bad news

When your partner gives you some bad news, use these expressions.

> Oh no!
> Unbelievable!

> You poor thing!
> I'm (very) sorry to hear that.

I lost all my bags when I traveled abroad.

Oh, you poor thing.

PRACTICE

Work with a partner. One is Student A; the other is Student B. Read the sentences below to your partner. Your partner will use one of the expressions above to react.

Student A

1. I've never had a vacation.

2. My bag was stolen on the beach in Hawaii.

3. The hotel made a mistake with my reservation. I had no room.

4. On my first day in Beijing, I spent all my money shopping and lost my passport.

Student B

1. I've never traveled to another city.

2. I broke my camera on my first day in Europe.

3. I missed my airplane, so I had to sleep in the airport.

4. The food I ate made me so sick.

Conversation listening

 A First listening

What places are the speakers talking about? Which are their favorites? Circle A or B.

1. The coolest place

   A  B

2. The most interesting place

   A  B

3. The most unbelievable place

   A  B

4. The best city in the world

   A  B

 B Second listening

What words or phases do they use to describe the places? Put checks (✔) in the boxes. You may check more than one box in each question.

1. ☐ humid ☐ beautiful scenery ☐ quiet ☐ gorgeous
2. ☐ windy ☐ crowded ☐ noisy ☐ delicious food
3. ☐ romantic ☐ historic places ☐ nice people ☐ polluted
4. ☐ expensive ☐ good food ☐ convenient ☐ great

 C Noticing the conversation strategies

Listen again for the expressions the speakers use to show surprise or react to bad news. Decide if the speakers like or dislike the place they visited. Put checks (✔) in the boxes.

	Like	Not so great
1.	☐	☐
2.	☐	☐
3.	☐	☐

Get ready!

Organize your questions, answers, and vocabulary here to get ready for your *Travel* conversation.

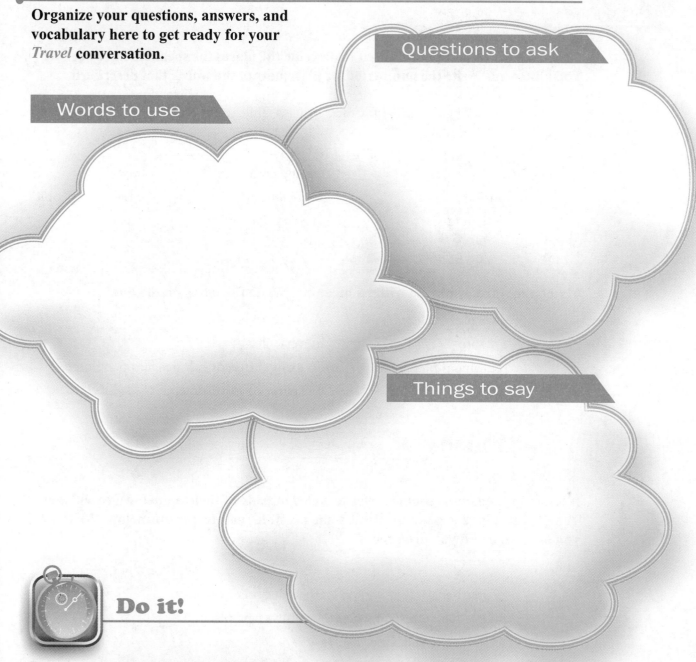

Questions to ask

Words to use

Things to say

Do it!

Practice some timed conversations with partners. When you hear something good, write it on this page after your conversation so you can remember it!

Noticing my partner's English

Real conversations

 A *Listening*

Check the words and phrases used to describe the places the speakers have been to. Then listen and write the number of the place next to the words that describe it.

(1) Laos	(2) Canada	(3) Chicago	(4) Chile	(5) New York

_____ beautiful mountains   _____ diversity   _____ hot

_____ busy   _____ freezing cold   _____ humid

_____ cheap food   _____ good night life   _____ interesting people

_____ nice restaurants   _____ historic buildings   _____ small

B *Vocabulary*

Match the word or phrase with its meaning. Write the letter on the line.

1. _____ diversity   a) of course
2. _____ for sure   b) very nice
3. _____ parliament buildings   c) many different cultures and people
4. _____ lovely   d) center of government

Thinking about . . .

Travel

A long time ago, most people never traveled outside of their hometown or village. Today, travel is very popular. Read some possible reasons for this below. Write **A** if you agree and **D** if you disagree.

Today . . .

1. _____ people believe they should learn about other cultures.
2. _____ people feel refreshed when they visit a new place.
3. _____ technology makes travel so easy.
4. _____ travel is a kind of entertainment.
5. _____ people travel to help the economy.
6. _____ travel experience gives us higher social status.

PRACTICE

Share your opinions with your partner. Remember to use the conversation strategies you have learned in previous units.

> I think people travel because they're curious about other people, food, and cultures.

> Really? I think travel is popular because it entertains people.

www.nicetalkingwithyou.com

Share your opinions with people your age. Listen to Global Voices to hear what English speakers around the world have to say.

Sports

Likes and dislikes

What sports do you like? Write on the lines below. Write L if you like the sport, D if you don't like it, and a question mark (?) if you aren't sure.

baseball	_____	skateboarding	_____
basketball	_____	skiing	_____
golf	_____	soccer	_____
lacrosse	_____	swimming	_____
rugby	_____	tennis	_____
running	_____	volleyball	_____

www.nicetalkingwithyou.com
Share your likes and dislikes with other people like you.

Words and phrases

Check the meaning of these words and phrases. Then use them to do the activities on the next page.

boring	flexible	once in a while	stiff	twice a week
competitive	go cycling	out of shape	stretch	warm up
difficult to learn	go hiking	play basketball	sweat	win
do aerobics	go skiing	play soccer	take lessons	work out
do exercise	in good shape	play tennis	learn sports	
easy to learn	lose	score	tied	
exciting	never	sometimes	tournament	

Match it

Match the word or phrase on the left with the meaning on the right. Write the letter on the line. Then check your answers with a partner.

1. _____ team sport

2. _____ win

3. _____ score

4. _____ work out

5. _____ tournament

6. _____ out of shape

a) final numbers of a game that show who won or lost

b) sports competition

c) do exercise, usually at a fitness center

d) someone who is not fit, who needs to exercise

e) a sport played or done with other people

f) opposite of lose

Fill it in

Use the words and phrases on page 67 to complete the sentences. Then check your answers with a partner.

1. I'd like to try snowboarding. I can already ski so it should be _____ _____ _____.

2. I'm so _____! I can't even reach my ankles when I bend down. I should _____ before I go to bed at night.

3. In the summer it's so hot! I have to carry a handkerchief to wipe the _____ away from my face.

4. Before we start soccer practice, we usually run around the track a few times to _____ _____.

5. I was in the tennis club when I was in high school, so I was _____ _____ _____. But now, since I never exercise, I get tired just walking up the stairs!

6. I don't like _____ _____ so much. I prefer noncompetitive sports.

7. The fans were disappointed because the final score was _____ at 7 to 7.

8. I used to go to the gym only _____ _____ _____ _____, but now I go twice a week.

Put it together

Draw a line to put the sentences together.

1. I like to watch   that I can do by myself.

2. I'm not so good   more free time.

3. I like sports activities   soccer games.

4. I would exercise if I had   at playing sports.

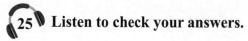 **Listen to check your answers.**

Conversation questions

> What sports do you like/play?
> Do you like . . . ?
> What kind of exercise do you do?

Practice asking and answering the questions above with different partners.

Watch out!

Be careful not to make these common mistakes!

✗	✔
~~Almost guys like soccer.~~	Most guys like soccer.
~~My body is not good condition.~~	I'm out of shape.
~~What is your best team?~~	What's your favorite team?

Practice saying these out loud so you can remember them.

Language point

play

I *play* soccer with my friends twice a week.

They *play* tennis most weekends.

go (+ verb-*ing*)

I *go swimming* whenever I can.

She *goes scuba diving* every year.

 PRACTICE

Complete the sentences. Write *play* or *go* on the lines below.

1. We _____ volleyball at the beach sometimes.

2. I _____ snowboarding or skiing every winter.

3. They _____ basketball once or twice a month.

4. I _____ running to get in shape.

5. We _____ hiking and camping in the summer.

6. I _____ baseball with my friends in the spring.

Conversation strategies

Making summary comments

Use the expressions below after your partner finishes talking about something. It shows you understand and that you are interested.

Reacting to something positive

> That's cool/nice/ good/great/interesting.

> Good for you!

Reacting to something negative

> That's too bad / a shame / terrible!

> I usually play baseball on the weekends.

> Our team won the competition!

> That's nice. Baseball is fun!

> Good for you! That's great!

PRACTICE

Read the sentences about sports below. Check (✔) five that you like. Read them to your partner. Use the expressions above when you hear your partner's sentences.

1. _____ I like skateboarding near the station with my friends.

2. _____ Our team came last in the competition.

3. _____ I don't exercise much, but I'm good at hip-hop dancing.

4. _____ I went bungee jumping last weekend.

5. _____ I broke my arm snowboarding last winter.

6. _____ I stretch every morning, and then I run two kilometers.

7. _____ I'm going bodyboarding at the beach tomorrow.

8. _____ I finally got my scuba diving license.

Showing little interest

If your partner asks you about something and you don't have a strong opinion, use one of the expressions below. (Don't say *So so*!)

It's OK.

It's all right.

It's not bad.

Do you like tennis?

Yeah, it's OK.

How about volleyball?

It's all right.

PRACTICE

Think of five sports or activities you think are just OK. Write them below.

Sport/Activity

1. _____
2. _____
3. _____
4. _____
5. _____

Now swap books with your partner. Take turns asking about the sports and activities. Answer using the expressions above.

What do you think of . . . ?

Do you like . . . ?

How about . . . ?

Conversation listening

 A First listening

Which sports do the speakers like the most? Circle A or B.

1. A    B

2. A    B

3. A    B

4. A    B

 B Second listening

Decide if the statements below are true or false. Write T if they are true and F if they are false.

1. The Eagles are a baseball team.   _____

2. You need a fast boat to pull a waterskier.   _____

3. Tennis is a sport for rich people.   _____

4. Basketball seems boring.   _____

 C Noticing the conversation strategies

Listen to how the speakers use the expressions (*It's*) *OK*, *It's all right*, **and** *It's not bad*. **Then decide which sport they are referring to. Circle A or B.**

1. **A** soccer   **B** baseball

2. **A** snow-skiing   **B** waterskiing

3. **A** golf   **B** tennis

4. **A** basketball   **B** baseball

Get ready!

Organize your questions, answers, and vocabulary here to get ready for your *Sports* conversation.

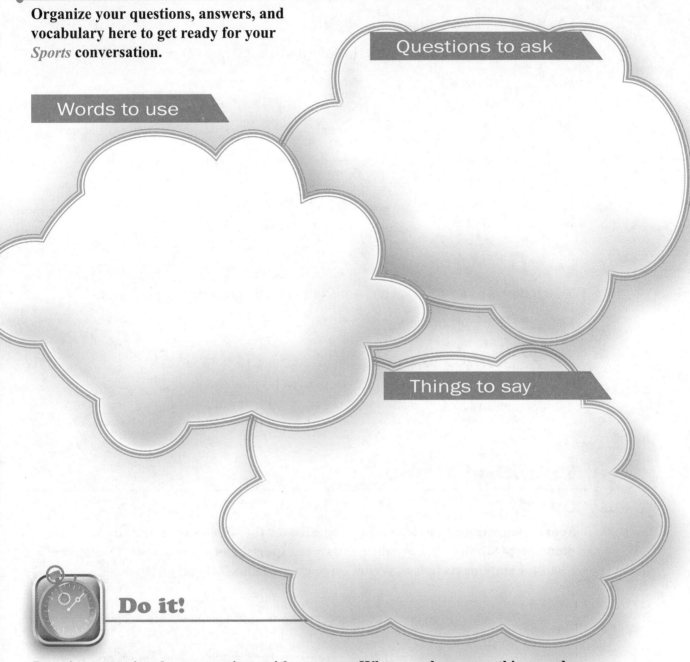

Questions to ask

Words to use

Things to say

Do it!

Practice some timed conversations with partners. When you hear something good, write it on this page after your conversation so you can remember it!

Noticing my partner's English

Real conversations

 A *Listening*

Match the sport or activity with the information the speaker gives about it.

1. _____ ice hockey
2. _____ cycling
3. _____ soccer
4. _____ going to the gym
5. _____ exercise
6. _____ running
7. _____ surfing
8. _____ walking

a) four or five times a week
b) broke her nose
c) likes to keep moving
d) the ultimate exercise
e) since the age of six
f) used to, but no time now
g) indoors, not outside
h) played goalie in high school

 B *Vocabulary*

Match the word or phrase with its meaning. Write the letter on the line.

1. _____ into something
2. _____ commute
3. _____ clear your head
4. _____ extreme sports
5. _____ injury
6. _____ keep yourself fit

a) a dangerous and exciting sport
b) keep your body healthy
c) damage to your body
d) really enjoy something
e) refresh your mind
f) travel from home to school or work

Thinking about . . .

Sports

Sports competitions have been popular all over the world for thousands of years. Some people, however, have little interest in sports, and some people dislike them. Read the statements below. Write A if you agree and D if you disagree.

1. _____ People need heroes, and athletes are natural heroes.
2. _____ Competition is a necessary part of human life, and sports help teach us to compete.
3. _____ Watching sports and playing sports are both activities that bring people together.
4. _____ Sports teams encourage fans to hate their rivals, which is bad for society.
5. _____ Sports prove how important teamwork is.
6. _____ Sports aren't really necessary. The world could live without them.

PRACTICE

Share your opinions with your partner. Remember to use the conversation strategies on pages 70 and 71.

> I don't think sports are necessary. I don't care who wins the gold medal in the Olympic Games.

> That's terrible! You should support your country!

www.nicetalkingwithyou.com
Share your opinions with people your age. Listen to Global Voices to hear what English speakers around the world have to say.

Friends

Likes and dislikes

Look at the list below. For each activity, write A if you enjoy doing it alone and F if you enjoy doing it with friends.

studying _____

working _____

shopping _____

traveling _____

going to a movie _____

going out to eat _____

singing karaoke _____

doing a sports activity _____

watching a sports game _____

playing video games _____

 www.nicetalkingwithyou.com

Share your likes and dislikes with other people like you.

Words and phrases

Check the meaning of these words and phrases. Then use them to do the activities on the next page.

a good listener	friend from	hang out together	moody	shy
ambitious	elementary school	impulsive	naive	smart
chatty	friend from high	interesting	nice	spacey
childhood friend	school	lazy	open-minded	the same age
crazy	gives me advice	live in the same	optimistic	thoughtful
onorgotio	grcat personality	neighborhood	pessimistic	trustworthy
fashionable	grow up together	meet often	popular	unique

Match it

Match the word on the left with the meaning on the right. Write the letter on the line. Check your answers with a partner.

1. _____ smart
2. _____ lazy
3. _____ pessimistic
4. _____ naive
5. _____ open-minded
6. _____ spacey

a) opposite of hardworking
b) inexperienced, innocent
c) not aware of what's happening around you
d) accepting new or different ways of thinking
e) intelligent
f) always thinking in negative ways

Fill it in

Use the words and phrases on page 75 to complete the sentences. Then check your answers with a partner.

1. She has a _____ _____. She's friendly and everybody likes her.

2. She's my friend from high school. We used to _____ _____ _____ all the time.

3. My best friend is very _____. Everyone likes him!

4. She's very _____! She always knows what to wear and always dresses great.

5. Ken wants to borrow my car for the weekend. Is he _____?

6. She's a nice person but sometimes she is so _____. Her personality changes all the time.

7. My best friend is really _____. She wants to be president of a big company one day!

8. He's a very interesting person and _____. Nobody in the world is like him.

Put it together

Draw a line to put the sentences together.

1. My best friend is   bit shy and quiet.
2. We've been friends   our personalities fit each other.
3. He's a little   since elementary school.
4. We get along because   called Jane.

28 **Listen to check your answers.**

Conversation questions

> Who's your best friend?
> What's he/she like?
> Why do you get along with him/her?

Practice asking and answering the questions above with different partners.

Watch out!

Be careful not to make these common mistakes!

✗

~~Keiko is my high school's friend.~~

~~She has shy character.~~

~~We don't meet recently.~~

✔

Keiko is my friend from high school.

She's shy.

We haven't seen each other for a long time.

Practice saying these out loud so you can remember them.

Language point

a little bit   kind of   very

My oldest friend is *a little bit* silly sometimes.

My sister is *kind of* crazy.

My friend from high school is *very* energetic.

PRACTICE

Use words from page 75 to complete the sentences below. Circle the words in *italics* to help describe the person.

1. My new friend is *a little bit / kind of / very* _____.

2. My oldest friend is *a little bit / kind of / very* _____.

3. My best friend is *a little bit / kind of / very* _____.

4. My friend from my neighborhood is *a little bit / kind of / very* _____.

Conversation strategies

Asking for an explanation

Sometimes your partner will use a word you don't know. Use this expression when you want to understand.

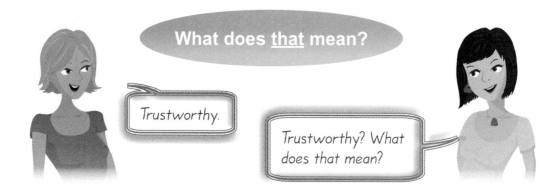

What does <u>that</u> mean?

Trustworthy.

Trustworthy? What does that mean?

Beginning an explanation

When you explain something, use the expression below if you think the word will be easy for your partner to understand.

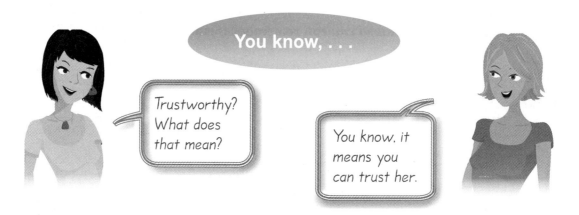

You know, . . .

Trustworthy? What does that mean?

You know, it means you can trust her.

Checking your partner understands

Use the expression below to check your partner understands.

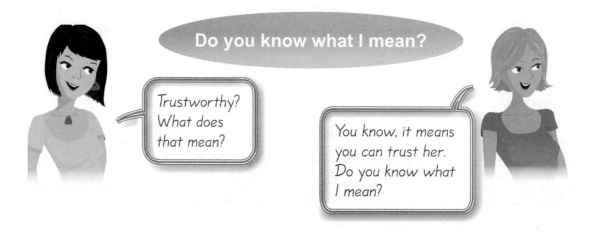

Do you know what I mean?

Trustworthy? What does that mean?

You know, it means you can trust her. Do you know what I mean?

Showing you understand

Use one of the expressions below to show you understand something.

> **I know what you mean.**

> **(Ah,) I see. I got it.**

You know, it means you can trust her. Do you know what I mean?

Yeah, I see. You can tell her a secret, and she won't tell anyone.

Right!!

PRACTICE

Work with a partner. One is Student A; the other is Student B. Look at your words below. Use a dictionary to check the meanings. Then choose four other words to explain. Write them on the lines.

Student A	Student B
rainbow	pregnant
thunder	aquarium
kitten	fireworks
nutritious	deadline
_____	_____
_____	_____
_____	_____
_____	_____

Explain the meaning of each word to your partner. You can use gestures or noises, but only English! Use the model below.

A: _____

B: _____? What does that mean?

A: You know, it means . . .

   Do you see what I mean?

B: Yeah, I see. / I know what you mean. / I got it.

Conversation listening

 A First listening

Listen to the four people talking about their friends. What words do they use to describe them? Put checks (✔) in the boxes.

1. Yoshi
2. Anita
3. Kim
4. Jin Hock

☐ patient	☐ interesting	☐ smart	☐ serious
☐ funny	☐ creative	☐ hardworking	☐ lazy
☐ energetic	☐ successful	☐ funny	☐ reliable

 B Second listening

Why do they get along well with their friend? Circle A or B.

1. **A** They've known each other since high school.
    B They are both a bit crazy.

2. **A** They are both curious.
    B They share an interest in fashion.

3. **A** They like the same kind of music.
    B They are both smart.

4. **A** They are both serious.
    B They are interested in the same social issues.

 C Noticing the conversation strategies

Listen to how the speakers ask for and offer explanations on the meanings of the words below. Then finish the sentences.

1. *Crazy* means entertaining and _____.
2. *Curious* means interested in _____ about new things.
3. *Spacey* means someone's body is here, but that person's _____ is somewhere out in space.
4. *Confident* means very _____ about your opinion.

Get ready!

Organize your questions, answers, and vocabulary here to get ready for your *Friends* conversation.

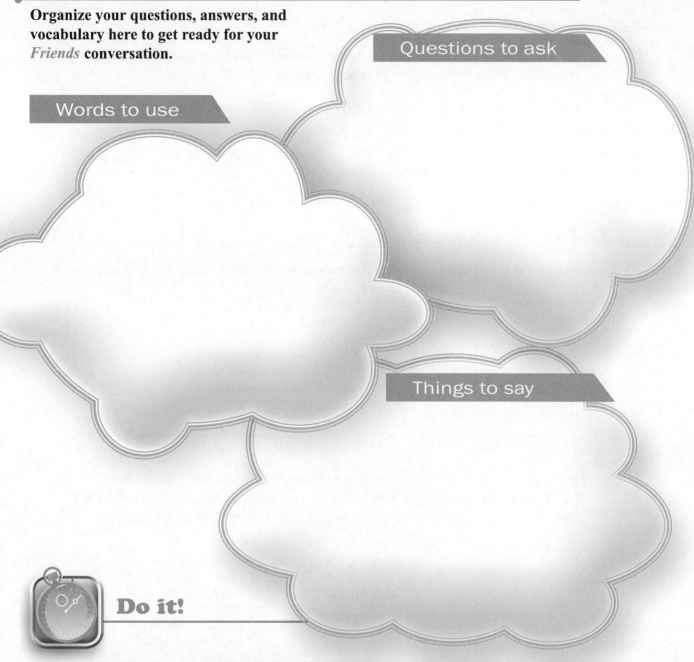

Words to use

Questions to ask

Things to say

Do it!

Practice some timed conversations with partners. When you hear something good, write it on this page after your conversation so you can remember it!

Noticing my partner's English

Real conversations

 A *Listening*

Listen to the speakers talk about their friends. Draw lines to match the names with the information the speakers give about them.

Shoko   always thinking about something

Graham   both like partying

James   very different, but they respect each other

Emily   likes fashion and shopping

Sebastian   both like traveling

 B *Vocabulary*

Match the word or phrase with the meaning. Write the letter on the line.

1. _____ sweet   a) interested in many different things

2. _____ awesome   b) confused, crazy

3. _____ inquisitive   c) kind, nice

4. _____ topsy-turvy   d) wonderful, amazing

Thinking about . . .

Friendship

Some people believe that technology is changing the meaning of the word "friend" and the idea of friendship. How much do you agree or disagree with the following statements? (1 means you strongly agree; 5 means you strongly disagree.)

1. Life is impossible without friends.   _____

2. Technology makes friendships stronger.   _____

3. You can't be real friends with someone you know only online.   _____

4. Robots could never replace humans as friends.   _____

 PRACTICE

Share your opinions with your partner. Remember to use the conversation strategies on pages 78 and 79.

> In the future, I think it will be possible to have an android for a friend.

> Android? What does that mean?

> It means, like, a robot.

> Ah, I see. Really? I think friendship is possible only between people.

www.nicetalkingwithyou.com
Share your opinions with people your age. Listen to Global Voices
to hear what English speakers around the world have to say.

Work

Likes and dislikes

**There are many reasons why people like work. Read the sentences below.
Put checks (✔) in the boxes below if you agree.**

I like work because . . .

☐ I can be with other people.

☐ I feel satisfied when I do a good job.

☐ I get money.

☐ my boss is easygoing.

☐ my job is fun.

☐ I work for a good company.

☐ my job lets me be creative.

☐ I have a great work atmosphere.

 www.nicetalkingwithyou.com
Share your likes and dislikes with other people like you.

Words and phrases

**Check the meaning of these words and phrases. Then use them to do the activities
on the next page.**

co-worker	interview	quit	work only on the
day off	job listings	rent	weekends
deadline	looking for a job	responsibility	work overtime
diligent	make money	résumé	work part-time
experience	meetings	salary	work the late shift
get a promotion	pay bills	spend money on	workaholic
get a raise	payday	stressful	
get fired	presentation	training	
hired	project	work full-time	

Match it

Match the word or phrase on the left with the meaning on the right. Write the letter on the line. Check your answers with a partner.

1. _____ get fired
2. _____ bills
3. _____ payday
4. _____ résumé
5. _____ job interview
6. _____ rent

a) money you have to pay for telephone, electricity, gas, etc.
b) the day you receive your salary
c) a formal meeting with a company to decide if you are right for a job
d) money you have to pay every month for the place you live in
e) a list of your past jobs, experience, and education
f) lose your job

Fill it in

Use the words and phrases on page 83 to complete the sentences. Then check your answers with a partner.

1. I'm going to _____ my job soon because I can't stand it anymore!

2. I've been working too hard this week! I really need a _____ _____.

3. The _____ is very good. I'm getting double what I was making before.

4. My brother is a senior. Right now he's _____ _____ _____ _____. I hope he can find a really good one.

5. Deadlines and projects make my job very _____. It's hard for me to relax.

6. I enjoy my job because I like all my _____. We have a lot of fun talking and working at the same time.

7. I'm nervous because I have to make a _____ in tomorrow's meeting.

8. I work so hard. It's time for me to _____ _____ _____ and a _____.

Put it together

Draw a line to put the sentences together.

1. I work part-time   money they pay.
2. I've been there for   my co-workers.
3. I like working with   about a year.
4. I don't like the   at a restaurant as a waiter.

🎧 **31** Listen to check your answers.

 ## Conversation questions

> Where do you work?
> How long have you been working there?
> What do you like about your job?
> What don't you like about your job?

Practice asking and answering the questions above with different partners.

 ## Watch out!

Be careful not to make these common mistakes!

✗	✔
~~I have a part-time job tonight.~~	I have to work (at my part-time job) tonight.
~~I retired my job.~~	I quit my job.
~~I work at convenience.~~	I work at a convenience store.

Practice saying these out loud so you can remember them.

 ## Language point

COST (money you need to buy something): **expensive** **cheap**

PAY/SALARY (money you get for work): **high** **low**

The dress was kind of *expensive*. It cost $300!

I think my pay is a little bit *low*. I get only $5 an hour.

PRACTICE

Circle the correct word in *italics*.

1. I got a 40% discount for this dress – it was *cheap / low*.

2. She works part time for about $1,000 per month. That's kind of *expensive / high*.

3. It's *expensive / high* to get it when it's new. Wait until it's on sale.

4. My salary is really *cheap / low*, because I'm new!

Conversation strategies

Doubling the question

In conversation, it is common to ask a question and then follow it immediately with another, related question. This helps make the question clear and not too direct.

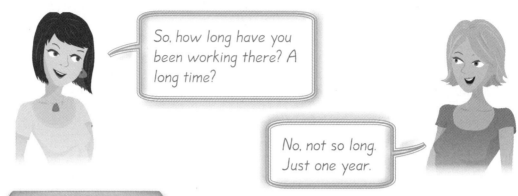

So, how long have you been working there? A long time?

No, not so long. Just one year.

PRACTICE

Match the double questions. Write the letter on the lines.

1. _____ How much do you make per hour?
2. _____ Do you get a lot of vacation time?
3. _____ Is it a fun place to work?
4. _____ What's your boss like?

a) More than three weeks?
b) Is it a lot?
c) Is she nice?
d) Good co-workers?

PRACTICE

Read the questions below and write another question on the line.

1. a) Do you like working there?

   b) _____

2. a) What are your co-workers like?

   b) _____

Guessing the next word

You can sometimes show your partner that you're listening carefully by guessing what he or she is going to say next.

Sometimes I'm late for work and my boss is very strict, so he . . .

Yells at you?

Yeah!

Oh, that's too bad.

PRACTICE

Work with a partner. One is Student A; the other is Student B. Look at the words and phrases below. Check you understand them. Then take turns reading the sentences below. Your partner will guess the word or phrase to finish the sentence.

I have to work, because I'm . . .

poor!

words/phrases			
at night	food	more money	speak English
fix their problems	interesting	so hard	strict

Student A

1. I like my job, but I just wish I could make . . .

2. My co-workers are nice, but our boss is very . . .

3. The place where I work isn't very busy – I don't have to work . . .

4. I don't like it when customers complain, because I can't usually . . .

Student B

1. I like the pay, but I don't like working so late . . .

2. Sometimes there are foreign customers, so I have a chance to . . .

3. I learn a lot of stuff at work. My job is . . .

4. It's good to work at a restaurant because sometimes you can get free . . .

Now write four words or phrases on the lines below. Make sentences like the ones above to explain them. Read them to your partner. Can your partner guess the word or phrase?

My word/phrase

1. _____
2. _____
3. _____
4. _____

My sentence

1. _____
2. _____
3. _____
4. _____

Conversation listening

 A First listening

Listen to the conversations about work. Number the pictures 1–4 in the order you hear about them. One is not used.

☐

☐

☐

☐

☐

 B Second listening

Why do the speakers like or dislike their jobs? Circle A, B, or C.

1. **A** good pay **B** likes co-workers **C** bad boss

2. **A** food is bad **B** cook isn't nice **C** man isn't nice

3. **A** boring **B** likes co-workers **C** noisy office

4. **A** convenient **B** good atmosphere **C** fun program

 C Noticing the conversation strategies

Listen again for the conversation strategies shown on page 86. Write the question that is doubled or the words that the speaker guesses.

Conversation	Doubling the question	Guessing the next word
1.		
2.		
3.		
4.		

Get ready!

Organize your questions, answers, and vocabulary here to get ready for your *Work* conversation.

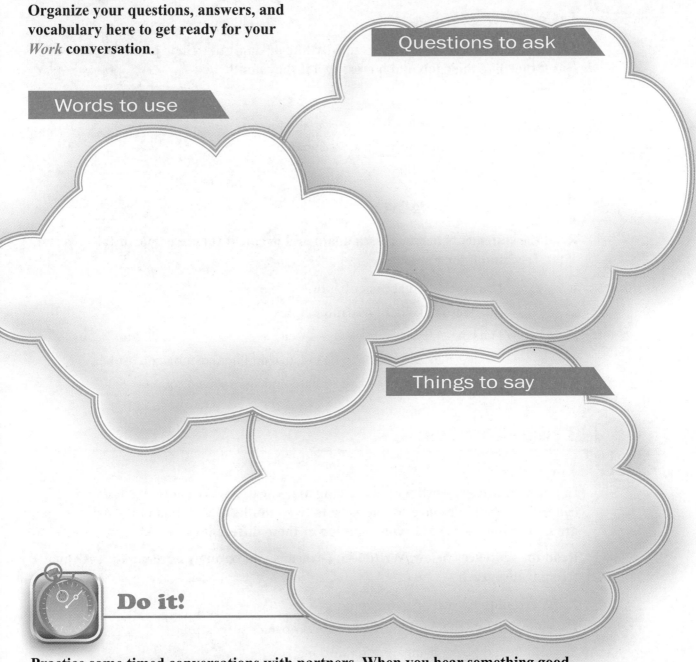

Words to use

Questions to ask

Things to say

Do it!

Practice some timed conversations with partners. When you hear something good, write it on this page after your conversation so you can remember it!

Noticing my partner's English

Real conversations

 A *Listening*

Listen and decide if the speakers mostly like or don't like their jobs. Put a check (✔) if they like their job and a cross (✘) if they don't.

1. ☐ working at a hotel
2. ☐ teaching children as a language assistant
3. ☐ teaching grammar to high school students
4. ☐ tailoring and modeling

33 **B** *True or false*

Read the statements below. Listen again and decide if they are true or false. Write T for True and F for False.

1. _____ The hotel job makes her happy.
2. _____ She doesn't like her boss at the hotel.
3. _____ The language assistant job pays well.
4. _____ Making suits allows her to be creative and her customers trust her.
5. _____ The delays make her work so hard and she wants to quit.

Thinking about . . .

Work

In many countries, work weeks are long and vacations are short. In some countries, companies give workers up to two months of vacation and work weeks are much shorter. What is your opinion of these different systems?

Read the sentences below. Write 1–5. (1 means you strongly agree; 5 means you strongly disagree.)

1. A two-month vacation is too long. _____
2. People must work hard to make their companies successful. _____
3. Life should be for living, not for working. _____
4. A good economy depends on hard work by the average person. _____

PRACTICE

Share your opinions with your partner. Remember to use the conversation strategies on page 86.

> I don't think that people should have to work for the economy.

> What do you mean?

> I mean that it should be opposite – that the economy should . . .

> The economy should work for people! Yeah, I know what you mean.

www.nicetalkingwithyou.com
Share your opinions with people your age. Listen to Global Voices
to hear what English speakers around the world have to say.

Movies

Likes and dislikes

Do you agree with the statements below? Write A if you agree and D if you disagree.

I like . . .

action movies more than romance. _____

comedies more than dramas. _____

women who are tough, not sensitive. _____

men who are intelligent, not macho. _____

women who are funny. _____

men who are handsome. _____

www.nicetalkingwithyou.com

Share your likes and dislikes with other people like you.

Words and phrases

Check the meaning of these words and phrases. Then use them to do the activities on the next page.

a loser	cute	intelligent	polite
action	drama	is fun to be with	romance
animation	feminine	macho	romantic
character	good at	make me laugh	sensitive
charming	handsome	masculine	sexy
childish	has a sense of humor	never gives up	stereotype
comedy	impolite	outgoing	strong
cool	intellectual	personality	tough

Match it

Match the word or phrase on the left with the meaning on the right. Write the letter on the line. Check your answers with a partner.

1. _____ personality
2. _____ character
3. _____ intellectual
4. _____ a loser
5. _____ feminine
6. _____ outgoing

a) someone who can't win, especially in romance
b) someone friendly and talkative
c) like a woman; opposite of masculine
d) the way you are as a person
e) interested in learning and thinking about complicated ideas
f) the qualities that make each person different

Fill it in

Use the words and phrases on page 91 to complete the sentences. Then check your answers with a partner. Some questions have more than one possible answer.

1. I loved that comedy. Some of the scenes _____ _____ _____ so much.

2. He played a _____ character. The character didn't want to grow up.

3. She's very _____ and romantic in the movie. Her character was very different from her last movie, when she was a tough action hero.

4. His acting was incredible. He was both macho and _____ at the same time.

5. I didn't know she _____ _____ _____ _____ _____ because she usually plays a serious character.

6. After all these years, he's still so _____.

7. James Bond is an action hero who is intelligent, charming and very, very _____. He's never afraid.

8. Indiana Jones is an action hero who is also _____. He's tough, but he also loves to study and read.

Put it together

Draw a line to put the sentences together.

1. I like romantic   are selfish.
2. *Avatar* is a really cool   movies, like *Titanic*.
3. I like male actors who are   science fiction movie.
4. I don't like female actors who   tough, but kind.

34 Listen to check your answers.

Conversation questions

> What kind of movies do you like?
> What kind of actor/actress do you like?
> Why do you like him/her?

Practice asking and answering the questions above with different partners.

 ## Watch out!

Be careful not to make these common mistakes.

✗	✔
~~I like action movie.~~	I like action movies.
~~I like macho man.~~	I like men who are strong/tough.
~~She is kind heart.~~	She's kind. / She has a kind heart.

Practice saying these out loud so you can remember them.

 ## Language point

kind (adjective)

I like people who are *kind*. / I like *kind* people.

kindness (noun)

Kindness is important.

intelligent (adjective)

She's really *intelligent*.

intelligence (noun)

Intelligence isn't everything.

PRACTICE

Circle the correct form of the words in *italics* below.

1. I think girls like guys who are *polite* / *politeness* to women.

2. Do you believe that women care about *honest* / *honesty* more than men?

3. Some couples are *affectionate* / *affection*, even in public.

4. No one likes *jealous* / *jealousy* in a relationship.

5. I think *romantic* / *romance* guys are cool!

Conversation strategies

Showing you are thinking

When you are not sure how to say something in English or are trying to remember a word, use the expression below. It will show your partner that you are thinking and need more time.

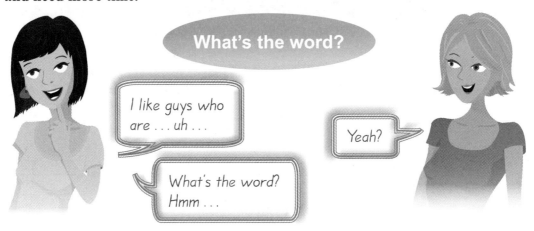

What's the word?

I like guys who are . . . uh . . .

What's the word? Hmm . . .

Yeah?

Getting time to think

If you need more time to think, use the expression below.

Give me a second.

If your partner says *Give me a second*, use the expressions below to show it's OK.

No problem!

Take your time.

What's the word? Hmm. Give me a second.

No problem! Take your time.

You know, it means he's never late to meet me. And he never forgets a special day . . .

Uh-huh.

Ah! Reliable! That's it. Guys who are reliable.

Ah, yeah. I see!

PRACTICE

Look at the words below. Write a sentence to explain each word. Then add two more words and write sentences to explain them.

	Word	Meaning
1.	reliable	someone who never forgets a special day
2.	brave	
3.	charming	
4.		
5.		

Work with a partner. Pretend you can't remember the words. Use the example on page 94 to help you.

Keeping the conversation going

In conversation, when you can't explain something, you can use this expression. It will keep the conversation going.

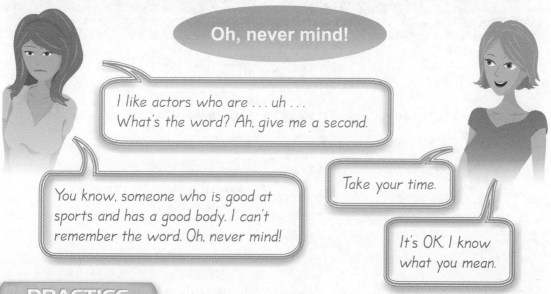

Oh, never mind!

I like actors who are . . . uh . . . What's the word? Ah, give me a second.

You know, someone who is good at sports and has a good body. I can't remember the word. Oh, never mind!

Take your time.

It's OK. I know what you mean.

PRACTICE

Write two words in the boxes below. Then write some notes to help you explain the meaning of the words in English. With your partner, have short conversations like the one above. Remember to use the conversation strategies on page 94 and the expression above.

	Word	Meaning
1.	athletic	strong; fit; good at sports
2.		
3.		

Conversation listening

 A First listening

Listen to the conversations about movies and decide what kind of movie the speakers watched. Number the posters 1–4 in the order you hear about them. One is not used.

B Second listening

What kind of people do the speakers like? Fill in the blanks below.

1. Someone who can make her _____.
2. Someone who is _____ and affectionate.
3. A hero who is brave and _____ , not afraid to take a chance.
4. Someone who makes him _____.

C Noticing the conversation strategies

In each of the conversations, there is some communication trouble. Listen again for the conversation strategies shown on pages 94 and 95. How do the speakers deal with the problem? Put checks (✔) in the boxes.

	1	2	3	4
a) The speaker can't find the right words, but the listener still understands.				
b) The speaker can't find the right words, and the listener can't understand.				
c) The speaker can't remember the word, but the listener helps.				

Get ready!

Organize your questions, answers, and
vocabulary here to get ready for your
Movies conversation.

Questions to ask

Words to use

Things to say

Do it!

Practice some timed conversations with partners. When you hear something good
your partner says, write on this page after your conversation so you can remember it!

Noticing my partner's English

Real conversations

A Listening

Listen to the speakers talk about actors or movie characters. Write 1–4 below in the order you hear the name of the actor or character.

a) _____ Elle Woods in *Legally Blonde*   c) _____ Brad Pitt

b) _____ Johnny Depp   d) _____ Russell Crowe in *Gladiator*

B Vocabulary

Match the words or phrases on the left with those on the right.

1. _____ girly, about love   a) brave
2. _____ intellectual   b) romantic
3. _____ charming, funny   c) strong
4. _____ beautiful, stylish   d) smart
5. _____ courageous   e) good fashion sense
6. _____ muscular, tough   f) artistic, different, not macho

Thinking about . . .

Movies

Some people say movies and TV programs give us an unrealistic view of the world. The women are beautiful and the men are heroes. Read the statements below. Write 1–5 below. (1 means you strongly agree; 5 means you strongly disagree.)

1. Movies influence our ideas about romance.   _____

2. Movies make it difficult for us to be happy with our lives.   _____

3. We often copy the behavior of the TV and movie characters we like.   _____

4. The impact of movies and TV is the same as stories in books or stories
   our parents tell us when we're kids.   _____

5. Society, not Hollywood, should control the messages we get from movies. _____

PRACTICE

Share your opinions with your partner. Remember to use the conversation strategies on pages 94 and 95.

> I don't think movies affect our thinking so much. It's possible to fall in love just like people do in the movies.

> But don't you think that these characters, I mean, um . . . what's the word?

> Take your time.

> Oh! I got it. Stereotypes. I think the stereotype characters in movies show us heroes that don't exist in real life!

www.nicetalkingwithyou.com

Share your opinions with people your age. Listen to Global Voices to hear what English speakers around the world have to say.

Personal tech

Likes and dislikes

What do you use technology for? How much do you use it? Write 1–5 below. (1 means you never use technology for this; 5 means you use technology for this all the time.)

I use technology for . . .

business communication.   _____   personal calls.   _____

getting news.   _____   reading.   _____

keeping a schedule.   _____   studying.   _____

listening to music.   _____   watching movies.   _____

looking at photos.   _____   writing.   _____

www.nicetalkingwithyou.com
Share your likes and dislikes with other people like you.

Words and phrases

Check the meaning of these words and phrases. Then use them to do the activities on the next page.

account	desktop	log in	read e-mails	storage
app	display	making videos	shopping	tablets
back up	gadget	memory	online	texting
blog	headset	monitor	smartphone	upload
chat	laptop	netbook	social network	user name
computer	light and	notebook	site	video chat
games	compact	password	spam	wireless

Match it

Match the word or phrase on the left with the meaning on the right. Write the letter on the line. Check your answers with a partner.

1. _____ smartphone
2. _____ gadget
3. _____ headset
4. _____ memory
5. _____ video chatting
6. _____ spam

a) seeing and talking to someone at the same time through the Internet
b) e-mail you don't want; junk e-mail
c) storage space on a gadget or computer
d) something you can use for e-mail, texting, watching videos, and calling people
e) something you wear and use to talk on the phone, listen to music, etc.
f) any personal electronic device, for example, an iPod

Fill it in

Use the words and phrases on page 99 to complete the sentences. Then check your answers with a partner.

1. I get ideas for cooking by reading different cooking _____.

2. I like _____ _____ for music and games. It's really convenient.

3. I need to get a new _____. I want to play games on a really big screen.

4. I _____ _____ at least a few times a day. I get sad when I don't get anything but _____.

5. I like to _____ photos from my digital camera to my home page.

6. The computer has changed my grandmother's life. She can _____ _____ with her grandchildren all over the world.

7. I forgot my _____! I need a better way to remember it.

8. I can't _____ _____ until I remember it!

Put it together

Draw a line to put the sentences together.

1. I have a computer   but I'd like to have one.
2. I've never used a tablet,   read books and news online.
3. I use my MP3 player   at home – it's a desktop.
4. I use my gadget to   every day, everywhere I go.

37 **Listen to check your answers.**

Conversation questions

> What kind of . . . do you have?
> Do you sometimes/often use a . . . ?
> What do you do with it?

Practice asking and answering the questions above with different partners.

Watch out!

Be careful not to make these common mistakes!

✘	✔
I using it every day.	I use it every day.
I want to get.	I want to get one/it.
I don't need.	I don't need one/it.

Practice saying these out loud so you can remember them!

Language point

still   (not) yet   already

I *still* have the old model.
(I had the old model before, and I have the old model now.)

I do*n't* have the new model *yet*.
(I don't have the new model, but I plan to get it.)

I *already* got the new model.
(The new model went on sale very recently. I have the new model.)

PRACTICE

Read the sentences below. Decide which is the correct word. Write it on the line.

1. I've been waiting for it, but I haven't gotten one _____.
2. Call to see if they _____ have them in stock, because maybe there are no more.
3. I think they're sold out _____. You're too late!
4. I don't have enough money _____, but when I do, I'll buy it.
5. Are you _____ using that old one? It's time to buy the new one!

Conversation strategies

Letting your partner raise a topic

When you start a conversation, you can use one of the questions below to invite your partner to talk about something.

(So,) What's new?   **(So,) What's up?**

So, what's new?

Nothing special.
But I caught a cold.

Oh, you poor thing.

So, what's up?

Nothing much.
What's new with you?

PRACTICE

Think of four different answers to the question *What's new?* (It's OK to make them up!)

Example: *I have a new cell phone.*

1. _____

2. _____

3. _____

4. _____

Now practice asking your partner *What's new?* or *What's up?* When your partner asks, use the answers you wrote.

Raising a related topic

To keep the conversation going, use the expression below to introduce new or related topics.

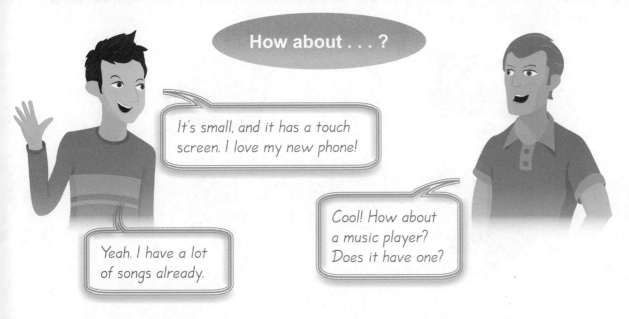

How about . . . ?

It's small, and it has a touch screen. I love my new phone!

Cool! How about a music player? Does it have one?

Yeah. I have a lot of songs already.

PRACTICE

Personal tech is a very broad topic. There's a lot to talk about. Look at the subtopics here. Add three more of your own in the columns below.

Describing gadgets	Using gadgets
size	Internet – for study
weight	e-mail – for work
display	games – for fun
_____	_____
_____	_____
_____	_____

Work with a partner. Choose some subtopics to talk about. Remember to use the conversation strategies. You can also use the double question strategy from Unit 10 on page 86.

1. How about the size? Is it really small?

2. How about the Internet? Do you use it a lot for your study?

3. How about the display? _____?

4. How about _____? _____?

5. How about _____? _____?

6. How about _____? _____?

A First listening

Listen to the conversations. Number the pictures in the order you hear about them. One is not used.

 B Second listening

What do the speakers use the items for? Circle the letters. You may circle more than one in each question.

1. **A** reading   **B** listening to music   **C** making calls

2. **A** making art   **B** writing programs   **C** playing games

3. **A** making calls   **B** watching videos   **C** writing reports

4. **A** sending e-mails **B** taking notes   **C** writing lectures

 C Noticing the conversation strategies

The speakers use the expression *How about . . . ?* to get more information about how the gadget can be used. Listen again and decide if they plan to use it for that purpose. Put checks (✔) in the boxes.

	Yes	No		Yes	No
1.	☐	☐	3.	☐	☐
2.	☐	☐	4.	☐	☐

Get ready!

Organize your questions, answers, and
vocabulary here to get ready for your
Personal tech conversation.

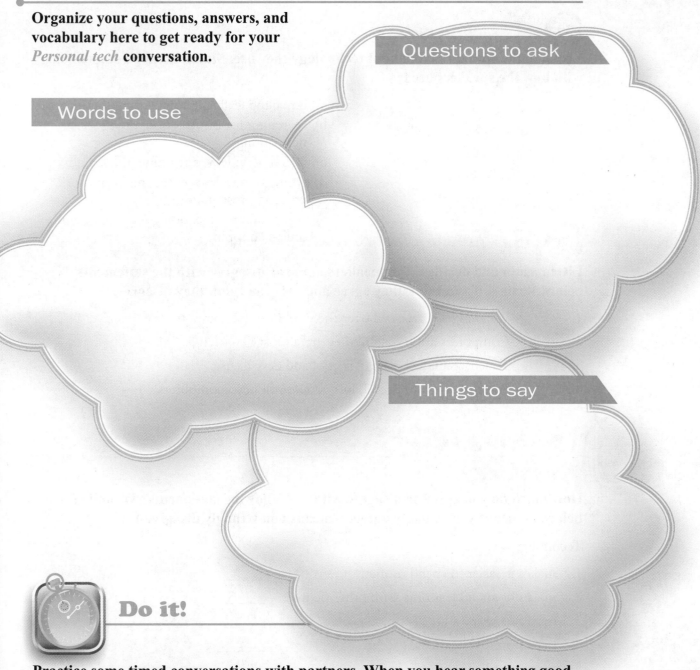

Questions to ask

Words to use

Things to say

Do it!

Practice some timed conversations with partners. When you hear something good,
write it on this page after your conversation so you can remember it!

Noticing my partner's English

Real conversations

A Listening

Listen to the speakers talk about technology they use. Match the type of technology with how the speakers use it.

1. _____ laptop
2. _____ desktop computer
3. _____ tablet
4. _____ cell phone
5. _____ smartphone

a) e-mailing, calling people, using the Internet
b) searching for information, doing social networking
c) watching videos, streaming TV online
d) typing documents, e-mailing homework, creating presentations
e) contacting people, doing graphic design, online shopping

B Agree or disagree

Listen again and decide if the speakers agree or disagree with the statements below. Write A if you think they agree and D if you think they disagree.

1. _____ Watching TV from all over the world on the computer is expensive.
2. _____ Computers are so useful they are almost like friends.
3. _____ Touchscreen technology is cool and easy to use.
4. _____ Smartphones are useful, but people still need computers.

Thinking about . . .

Technology

How much do you agree or disagree with the following statements? Write 1–5 below. (1 means you strongly agree; 5 means you strongly disagree.)

Technology . . .

1. makes it easier to spend money.   _____
2. makes us spend less time with other people.   _____
3. makes us waste a lot of time.   _____
4. makes our lives easier.   _____
5. makes our lives better.   _____

PRACTICE

Share your opinions with your partner. Remember to use the conversation strategies you have learned in previous units.

> I don't think all this technology makes us more productive.

> Productive? What does that mean?

> Like helping us do things better or faster. I mean, now I spend all my time charging gadgets and making sure everything is organized correctly.

> How about your smartphone? Do you really think you can live without that?

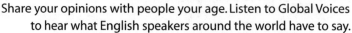

www.nicetalkingwithyou.com

Share your opinions with people your age. Listen to Global Voices to hear what English speakers around the world have to say.

Review 2

Conversation strategies

Unit 7

You're kidding!
Oh my gosh!
You're lucky!
I'm so jealous!
Oh no!
Unbelievable!
You poor thing!
I'm (very) sorry to hear that.

Unit 8

That's cool/nice/good/great/interesting.
Good for you!
That's too bad / a shame / terrible!
It's OK / all right / not bad.

Unit 9

What does <u>that</u> mean?
You know, . . .

Do you know what I mean?
I know what you mean.
(Ah,) I see. I got it.

Unit 10

Doubling the question
Guessing the next word

Unit 11

What's the word?
Give me a second.
No problem!
Take your time.
Oh, never mind!

Unit 12

(So,) What's new?
(So,) What's up?
How about . . . ?

A. Take turns reading the sentences and guessing the next word.

Sports

Sentence	Word to guess
I like fast sports like tennis and soccer and	*basketball*
I don't really like slow sports like golf or	

Work

Sentence	Word to guess
My job is OK but I don't like it when the boss gets	
My job would be better if I could get a longer	

B. Fill in the boxes with sentences to say to your partner and a word you think they will easily guess! Then take turns reading the sentences and guessing the word.

Friends

Sentence	Word to guess

Travel

Sentence	Word to guess

LISTENING PRACTICE 1

Listen to three conversations. In each conversation there is a communication problem: the speaker can't find the word or words to explain something. But they still keep talking.

The problems in the conversations are handled in three different ways:

a) The speaker can't find the words, and the listener doesn't understand.

b) The speaker can find enough words to explain and the listener can understand.

c) The speaker can't remember the word, but the listener helps.

40 **Listen to each conversation. Match the descriptions above with the correct conversation. Write a, b, and c on the correct lines below.**

Conversation 1 _____   Conversation 2 _____   Conversation 3 _____

SPEAKING PRACTICE 2

In Unit 10, you learned to use the strategy of doubling the question, and in Unit 12 you learned how to keep a conversation going by using *How about . . . ?* You can put these two strategies together.

Example:

How about Chinese food? What's your favorite dish?

Fill in the chart below. Complete a *How about . . . ?* question about each topic. Then write the second question for each topic.

Topic	How about . . . ?	Second question
Travel	*How about Palau?*	*Have you ever been there?*
Sports	*How about . . . ?*	
Friends		
Work		
Movies		
Personal tech		

Now practice with a partner to make conversations like the one below.

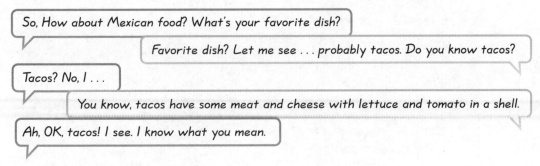

So, How about Mexican food? What's your favorite dish?

Favorite dish? Let me see . . . probably tacos. Do you know tacos?

Tacos? No, I . . .

You know, tacos have some meat and cheese with lettuce and tomato in a shell.

Ah, OK, tacos! I see. I know what you mean.

A. Listen to two conversations. You will hear the speakers using different conversation strategies in each. Some of the expressions they use are written below. Listen and write other expressions you hear.

Conversation 1	Conversation 2
How's it going?	Oh my gosh!

B. Listen again, and to one more conversation. In which conversation do the speakers use the strategies below? Put checks (✔) in the boxes.

Strategy	Conversation 1	Conversation 2	Conversation 3
Guessing the word			
Doubling the question			
Reacting to bad news			

Conversation strategies

Unit 1
How's it going? / How are you doing?

Great! / Good! / Pretty good.

OK. / Not bad. / All right.

Not so good.

Nice talking with you!

How about you?

Pardon me? / Excuse me?

Unit 2
Hmm . . . Let me see.

Hmm . . . Let me think.

That's a good/difficult question.

Unit 3
Oh, really?

Oh, yeah?

Uh-huh.

Mm-hmm.

So, . . .

Unit 4
Me too.

I do too.

Me neither.

I don't either.

Really? I don't.

Really? I do.

What else?

Unit 5
Like what?

Like who?

For example?

Tripling your reaction

Unit 6
. . . and stuff.

. . . and stuff like that.

. . . or something?

Unit 7
You're kidding!

Oh my gosh!

You're lucky!

I'm so jealous!

Oh no!

Unbelievable!

You poor thing!

I'm (very) sorry to hear that.

Unit 8
That's cool/nice/good/great/interesting.

Good for you!

That's too bad / a shame / terrible!

It's OK / all right / not bad.

Unit 9
What does <u>that</u> mean?

You know, . . .

Do you know what I mean?

I know what you mean.

(Ah,) I see. I got it.

Unit 10
Doubling the question

Guessing the next word

Unit 11
What's the word?

Give me a second.

No problem!

Take your time.

Oh, never mind!

Unit 12
(So,) What's new?

(So,) What's up?

How about . . . ?

Answers

Unit 1

Match it

1. e)   3. f)   5. b)
2. a)   4. c)   6. d)

Fill it in

1. part-time job   5. by myself
2. born   6. rural
3. free time   7. favorite
4. am interested in   8. school / work

Put it together

1. My name is Veronica. It's nice to meet you.
2. I was born in Australia, but I'm from China.
3. My name is Kazutoshi, so please call me Toshi.
4. I'm interested in travel and playing the piano.
5. I like TV and watching sports like soccer and tennis.

Language point

have 3   *are* 2
is 5   *will* 4
am 1

Conversation listening

A. First listening

a) 1   c) not used   e) 4
b) 3   d) 2

B. Second listening

1. B   3. A
2. A   4. B

C. Noticing the conversation strategies

1. B   3. A
2. A   4. A

Real conversations

A. Listening

1. c)   3. d)
2. e)   4. a)

B. True or false

1. T
2. F (10 months not 10 years)
3. T
4. T

Unit 2

Match it

1. d)   4. a)
2. e)   5. c)
3. f)   6. b)

Fill it in

1. an only child
2. is like
3. am different from
4. the middle child
5. talkative
6. strict
7. easygoing
8. pets

Put it together

1. There are five people in my family.
2. I have a big family.
3. My father is not so tall and a little bit fat.
4. I get along well with my mother.

Language point

1. There are
2. There is
3. There are

4. There are

5. There is

Conversation listening

A. First listening

(pictures numbered clockwise from top left)

Picture 1 (grandmother): 2

Picture 2 (bald dad): 4

Picture 3 (brother): 1

Picture 5 (smart sister): 3

B. Second listening

1. average
3. smart

2. sweet
4. bald

C. Noticing the conversation strategies

a) 2
d) 3

b) 1
e) not used

c) 4

Real conversations

A. Listening

a) 6
e) 5

b) 4
f) 1

c) 2
g) 7

d) 3

B. Vocabulary

1. c)
4. a)

2. e)
5. b)

3. d)

Unit 3

Match it

1. b)
3. d)
5. c)

2. f)
4. e)
6. a)

Fill it in

1. guarantee
5. try something on

2. window-shopping
6. retail outlets

3. brand-name
7. discount

4. go with a friend
8. impulse buyer

Put it together

1. I like shopping very much.

2. I don't like shopping at all.

3. I go shopping about once a week.

4. I like shopping for clothes and games and DVDs.

Language point

1. much
4. much

2. many
5. many

3. many

Conversation listening

A. First listening

1. A
3. B

2. A
4. B

B. Second listening

1. B
3. B

2. B
4. A

C. Noticing the conversation strategies

1. Woman
3. Man

2. Man
4. Woman

Real conversations

A. Listening

a) 4
d) 3

b) 1
e) 2

c) 5

B. Vocabulary

1. d)
3. a)

2. c)
4. b)

Unit 4

Match it

1. e)
3. f)
5. a)

2. d)
4. b)
6. c)

Fill it in

1. good for you;
   too many calories
2. go out to eat
3. snack
4. portions

5. spicy
6. leftovers
7. on a diet;
   fast food
8. delicious/
   yummy

Put it together

1. I like many kinds of food.
2. I like it because it's sweet.
3. I eat it almost every day.
4. I don't like it because it tastes bitter.

Language point

1. Why not?
2. Why not?
3. Why?

4. Why not?
5. Why?

Conversation listening

A. First listening

(*Pictures numbered from top to bottom, left to right*)

Picture 1: 3
Picture 2: 1
Picture 3: 4

Picture 4: not used
Picture 5: 2

B. Second listening

1. bitter
2. spicy

3. crisp
4. healthy

C. Noticing the conversation strategies

1. D
2. A
3. A

4. D
5. D
6. A

7. A

Real conversations

A. Listening

L seafood

L pasta

D vegetables

D fast food

L meat and potatoes

L junk food

L Thai food

D mushrooms

D/L cucumbers

L tomatoes

B. Vocabulary

1. c)
2. d)

3. e)
4. a)

5. b)

Unit 5

Match it

1. f)
2. e)

3. b)
4. a)

5. c)
6. d)

Fill it in

Note: Some questions may have more than one answer.

1. loud
2. singer
3. soundtrack
4. musical
   instruments

5. live concert
6. soft / slow
7. rhythm
8. find out about;
   download

Put it together

1. I love hip-hop music – it's great to dance to.
2. I practice guitar and I like playing rock music.
3. I listen to Beyoncé – I have all of her music.
4. I don't like classical music – I think it's boring.

Language point

Many examples possible, e.g., "Do you know 'Only Girl' by Rihanna? Her music is very popular."

Conversation listening

A. First listening

(*Pictures numbered from top to bottom, left to right*)

Picture 1: 2
Picture 2: not used
Picture 3: 3

Picture 4: 1
Picture 5: 4

B. Second listening

1. Ballads (relaxing)

2. Dance music (cheers you up)

3. Punk and metal (gives me energy)

4. Pop (lets me be creative)

C. Noticing the conversation strategies

1. B   3. A

2. A   4. A

Real conversations

A. Listening

L R&B / hip-hop

D house

L Japanese visual music

L British indie music

L K-Pop

L classical

L rock

D rap

B. Vocabulary

1. d)   3. e)   5. c)

2. a)   4. b)

Unit 6

Match it

1. e)   3. a)   5. c)

2. d)   4. f)   6. b)

Fill it in

1. meeting new people

2. reading books

3. Going to restaurants

4. surfing the Internet

5. Taking weekend trips

6. Taking photos

7. relaxing at home

8. get rid of stress

Put it together

1. In my free time I like reading books.

2. I don't have a hobby these days.

3. When I was young, I used to collect sports cards.

4. No, I've never tried bungee jumping.

Language point

1. play   4. making

2. Watching   5. use

3. do

Conversation listening

A. First listening

1. B   3. B
2. B   4. A

B. Second listening

1. A   3. C
2. B   4. A

C. Noticing the conversation strategies

1. A   3. B
2. A   4. B

Real conversations

A. Listening

12 belly dancing

14 bungee jumping

8 cooking

1 designing fashion

11 drinking coffee

10 eating cakes

4 hanging out with friends

7 Internet surfing

6 photography

2 reading

5 skateboarding

13 skydiving

9 swimming

3 walking

B. Vocabulary

1. f)   3. a)   5. c)

2. e)   4. b)   6. d)

Review 1

LISTENING PRACTICE 1

Conversation 1: b)

Conversation 2: c)

Conversation 3: a)

LISTENING PRACTICE 2

A

Conversation 1	Conversation 2
How's it going?	So, . . .
Pretty good.	Let me see.
Nice to meet you.	Mm-hmm.
Me too.	Like what?
That's a difficult question.	Oh yeah?
Me neither.	How about you?

B

Getting time to think: Conversations 1 and 2

Asking for examples: Conversation 2

Agreeing: Conversation 1

Unit 7

Match it

1. b)   3. e)   5. d)

2. f)   4. a)   6. c)

Fill it in

1. on a package tour
2. popular tourist destination
3. souvenirs
4. two nights and three days
5. breakfast buffet
6. beaches
7. nice view
8. airfares / rates

Put it together

1. I have traveled abroad only one time, to Canada.

2. I haven't been to Europe yet, but I want to go.

3. Australia was a really great place to visit.

4. It was my first time to go on an airplane.

Language point

1. traveled   4. flown
2. eaten   5. tried
3. held

Conversation listening

A. First listening

1. A   3. A
2. A   4. A

B. Second listening

1. beautiful scenery, gorgeous
2. crowded, noisy
3. historic places, nice people
4. good food, great

C. Noticing the conversation strategies

1. Like
2. Not so great
3. Like

Real conversations

A. Listening

(1) Laos   (4) Chile

(2) Canada   (5) New York

(3) Chicago

1 beautiful mountains

5 busy

1 cheap food

2 clean (Toronto)

2 diversity (Montreal)

3 freezing cold

2 good night life (Montreal)

2 historic buildings (Quebec City)

4 hot

4 humid

4 interesting people

1 small

B. Vocabulary

1. c)   3. d)
2. a)   4. b)

Unit 8

Match it

1. e)   3. a)   5. b)
2. f)   4. c)   6. d)

Fill it in

1. easy to learn   5. in good shape
2. stiff; stretch   6. team sports
3. sweat   7. tied
4. warm up   8. once in a while

Put it together

1. I like to watch soccer games.
2. I'm not so good at playing sports.
3. I like sports activities that I can do by myself.
4. I would exercise if I had more free time.

Language point

1. play   3. play   5. go
2. go   4. go   6. play

Conversation listening

A. First listening

1. A   2. A   3. A   4. A

B. Second listening

1. F   2. T   3. F   4. F

C. Noticing the conversation strategies

1. A (soccer)
2. B (waterskiing)
3. A (golf)
4. A (basketball)

Real conversations

A. Listening

1. e)   4. f)   7. b)
2. d)   5. a)   8. c)
3. h)   6. g)

B. Vocabulary

1. d)   3. e)   5. c)
2. f)   4. a)   6. b)

Unit 9

Match it

1. e)   3. f)   5. d)
2. a)   4. b)   6. c)

Fill it in

1. great personality   5. trustworthy
2. hang out together   6. moody
3. popular   7. ambitious
4. fashionable   8. unique

Put it together

1. My best friend is called Jane.
2. We've been friends since elementary school.
3. He's a little bit shy and quiet.
4. We get along because our personalities fit each other.

Language point

Example: My new friend is very impulsive.

Conversation listening

A. First listening

1. funny, energetic   3. smart
2. interesting, creative 4. serious

B. Second listening

1. B   3. A
2. B   4. B

C. Noticing the conversation strategies

1. fun   3. brain
2. learning   4. sure

Real conversations

A. Listening

Shoko: both like partying

Graham: both like traveling

James: always thinking about something

Emily: very different, but they respect each other

Sebastian: likes fashion and shopping

B. Vocabulary

1. c)   3. a)
2. d)   4. b)

Unit 10

Match it

1. f)   3. b)   5. c)
2. a)   4. e)   6. d)

Fill it in

1. quit   5. stressful
2. day off   6. co-workers
3. salary   7. presentation
4. looking for a job   8. get a promotion; raise

Put it together

1. I work part-time at a restaurant as a waiter.
2. I've been there for about a year.
3. I like working with my co-workers.
4. I don't like the money they pay.

Language point

1. cheap   3. expensive
2. high   4. low

Conversation strategies

(*Match the double questions. Write the letter on the lines.*)

1. b)   3. d)
2. a)   4. c)

Conversation listening

A. First listening

(*pictures numbered from top to bottom, left to right*)

Picture 1: not used   Picture 4: 4
Picture 2: 2   Picture 5: 1
Picture 3: 3

B. Second listening

1. B   3. A
2. C   4. B

C. Noticing the conversation strategies

1. Guessing the next word: ". . . like it, eh?"
2. Doubling the question: "Where do you work? Somewhere nearby?"
3. Doubling the question: "Oh, the one in the big tower, near the station? The new building?"
4. Guessing the next word: "computer . . . programming"

Real conversations

A. Listening

1. ×   3. √
2. √   4. √

B. True or false

1. F   4. T
2. T   5. F
3. F

Unit 11

Match it

1. d)   3. e)   5. c)
2. f)   4. a)   6. b)

Fill it in

1. made me laugh
2. childish
3. charming / cute / feminine / sensitive / sexy
4. sensitive
5. had a sense of humor
6. handsome
7. cool
8. intellectual

Put it together

1. I like romantic movies, like *Titanic*.
2. *Avatar* is a really cool science fiction movie.
3. I like male actors who are tough, but kind.
4. I don't like female actors who are selfish.

Language point

1. polite

2. honesty

3. affectionate

4. jealousy

5. romantic

Conversation listening

A. First listening

(pictures numbered from left to right, top to bottom)

Picture 1: 1 (comedy)

Picture 2: 3 (sci-fi)

Picture 3: 4 (documentary)

Picture 4: not used

Picture 5: 2 (romance)

B. Second listening

1. laugh   3. strong

2. romantic   4. think

C. Noticing the conversation strategies

1. c)   3. b)

2. a)   4. a)

Real conversations

A. Listening

a) 2   c) 4

b) 1   d) 3

B. Vocabulary

1. b)   4. e)

2. d)   5. a)

3. f)   6. c)

Unit 12

Match it

1. d)   3. e)   5. a)

2. f)   4. c)   6. b)

Fill it in

1. blogs

2. shopping online

3. display /desktop / monitor

4. read e-mails; spam

5. upload

6. video chat

7. password

8. log in

Put it together

1. I have a computer at home – it's a desktop.

2. I've never used a tablet, but I'd like to have one.

3. I use my MP3 player every day, everywhere I go.

4. I use my gadget to read books and news online.

Language point

1. yet   4. yet

2. still   5. still

3. already

Conversation listening

(pictures numbered from top to bottom, left to right)

A. First listening

Picture 1: 2

Picture 2: 4

Picture 3: 1

Picture 4: 3

Picture 5: not used

B. Second listening

1. B & C   3. B & C

2. A   4. A & B

C. Noticing the conversation strategies

1. Yes   3. Yes

2. No   4. Yes

Real conversations

A. Listening

1. c)   4. a)

2. e)   5. b)

3. d)

B. Agree or disagree

1. D   3. A

2. A   4. D

Review 2

LISTENING PRACTICE 1

Conversation 1: b)

Conversation 2: c)

Conversation 3: a)

LISTENING PRACTICE 2

A

Conversation 1	**Conversation 2**
How's it going?	Oh my gosh!
How about you?	That's so great.
That's nice.	Good for you.
What else . . . ?	That's terrible.
That sounds really great.	How about . . . ?

B

Guessing the word: Conversations 2 and 3

Doubling the question: Conversation 2

Reacting to bad news: Conversation 2

Note that Conversation 1 does not highlight any of the three strategies.